# Voices from the Mississippi Hill Country

# VOICES FROM THE MISSISSIPPI HILL COUNTRY

## The Benton County Civil Rights Movement

Roy DeBerry, Aviva Futorian, Stephen Klein, and John Lyons

University Press of Mississippi / Jackson

The University Press of Mississippi is the scholarly publishing agency of
the Mississippi Institutions of Higher Learning: Alcorn State University,
Delta State University, Jackson State University, Mississippi State University,
Mississippi University for Women, Mississippi Valley State University,
University of Mississippi, and University of Southern Mississippi.

www.upress.state.ms.us

The University Press of Mississippi is a member
of the Association of University Presses.

First printing 2020

∞

Library of Congress Cataloging-in-Publication Data

Names: DeBerry, Roy, author. | Futorian, Aviva, author. | Klein, Stephen,
1936- author. | Lyons, John, 1981- author.
Title: Voices from the Mississippi Hill Country: The Benton County Civil
Rights Movement / Roy DeBerry, Aviva Futorian, Stephen Klein, and John
Lyons.
Description: Jackson: University Press of Mississippi, [2020] | Includes
bibliographical references and index.
Identifiers: LCCN 2020007605 (print) | LCCN 2020007606 (ebook) | ISBN
9781496828828 (hardback) | ISBN 9781496828811 (trade paperback) | ISBN
9781496828835 (epub) | ISBN 9781496828842 (epub) | ISBN 9781496828859
(pdf) | ISBN 9781496828866 (pdf)
Subjects: LCSH: African AmericansCivil rightsHistoryInterviews. |
Benton County (Miss.)HistoryInterviews. | BISAC: SOCIAL SCIENCE /
Discrimination | LCGFT: Interviews.
Classification: LCC F347.B4 D43 2020 (print) | LCC F347.B4 (ebook) | DDC
976.2/89dc23
LC record available at https://lccn.loc.gov/2020007605
LC ebook record available at https://lccn.loc.gov/2020007606

British Library Cataloging-in-Publication Data available

# Contents

# Preface

You can drive through Benton County in the north hill country of Mississippi and never know it. Fewer than nine thousand people are scattered over four hundred square miles. Benton is among the poorest counties in America's poorest state. It has little industry, scarce entertainment, and very few jobs. There's not much beyond farms, forests, and two US highways.

But the thousands of travelers on US Highways 72 and 78 who drive through Benton County every day never realize they're passing through an area with one of the country's richest civil rights histories. Local chapters of the NAACP and a Citizens Club were organized in the 1940s and '50s. Benton was one of the first Mississippi counties to get a federal observer under the 1964 Voting Rights Act, it had the highest per capita percentage of registered voters, and its citizens produced a regular, clandestinely distributed newsletter called the *Benton County Freedom Train*.

This is a book about life before, during, and after the civil rights movement, as told in their own words by the residents of a rural county in northern Mississippi. It examines one of the most revolutionary periods in American history through the voices of farmers, teachers, sharecroppers, and students. Rather than the polished words of the movement's icons, we hear the simple eloquence of an elderly woman recalling her long days toiling in the cotton fields. We hear the courage of a sharecropper remembering voting for the first time. We hear the determination of parents deciding to send their children to integrate an all-white school. We hear the terror in a first-grader's voice, walking into an all-white classroom on the first day of school. We hear the resolve in a janitor recalling his first civil rights meeting. And we hear the wisdom and grace of a community talking about justice, equity, and the promise of a better future.

Through these first-person stories, covering more than a century's worth of history, we are presented with a vivid picture of these people, this place, and these times. In this book, Benton County residents, black and white, young and old, tell us in their voices about the events that shaped their lives and ultimately, in their own humble way, the trajectory of America.

Henry Reaves (standing) with Ellie Steward (center) and Rebecca Dorse (left), Samuel's Chapel, March 16, 1965. Courtesy of Aviva Futorian.

# Dedication

Henry Reaves, 1900–1990

*Voices from the Mississippi Hill Country* is about the power of a community working together. But one man, Henry Reaves, was the driving force behind the local movement's progress. Mr. Reaves's energy and commitment to change provided an invaluable contribution to the vibrant and productive civil rights movement in Benton County.

Born in 1900 to Levi Reaves and Jane MacDonald Reaves, he was home-schooled. When he was a young boy in the first years of the twentieth century, a time when illiteracy was by far the norm, Mr. Reaves's mother taught him how to read and write. Decades later, he saw in the school system one of the main battlegrounds of the movement, and was instrumental in organizing and encouraging black parents to send their children to integrate the school system. His children, Henry Jr. (Sonny) and Naomi, both did.

Well before the arrival of civil rights volunteers in 1964, Mr. Reaves was organizing residents in Benton County, largely around voting rights. He would visit every person on their twenty-first birthday (previously the eligibility age for voting) and speak to them about registering to vote. He was highly respected in the black community, so much so that when a young person who hadn't yet registered would see Mr. Reaves in town, they would run in the other direction to avoid having to confess their failure to him.

Mr. Reaves founded a local chapter of the NAACP and called it the Benton County Citizens Club. He visited churches in the county, talking about the importance of "being a citizen" through voting. Many of the interviewees credit Mr. Reaves with emboldening them to register and exercising the rights of citizenship. He traveled around the state, meeting with other organizations and activists. In the decades prior to the 1960s, it was incredibly lonely, dangerous work.

In the young people of Benton County, he saw the key to the movement. He would frequently drive young people to and from civil rights meetings around the state. Mr. Reaves also was a believer in self-reliance. He was a landowner, like most of the active members of the movement in Benton County. As his adopted nephew Henry Leake told us,

> He wouldn't let us work for white folks. He never said why. He just always showed us that you work for yourself.

Mr. Reaves passed away in 1990, before he could participate in this project. His work and legacy are clearly reflected in the lives of the people whose voices we recorded. He was a humble, independent farmer, born at the height of Jim Crow in a tiny, rural Mississippi county. Through dogged persistence, profound moral clarity, and sheer force of will, he led the people of Benton County, all of them, to a better future. Every county in America should be so fortunate.

# Introduction: Historical Context

Benton County is an area that is overlooked in many of America's civil rights histories. To that end, some historical context of this area may be of interest to the reader.

Benton County has remained sparsely populated, geographically isolated, and economically depressed for the entirety of its existence. Several decades ago, the population peaked at twelve thousand. Blacks have always been a significant minority, never comprising more than 47 percent of its citizenry. Today, the county has approximately eight thousand people, 40 percent of whom are black. Almost all of its residents, black and white, are poor, with a per capita income of $15,000, about half the national average and well below the state's modest average of $22,500.[1]

## Formative Years

The human history of the land that would become Benton County dates back thousands of years. The original inhabitants of that land were Chickasaw people, whose domain stretched from northern Mississippi through Tennessee and into Kentucky. When the first Europeans arrived, they saw the land's potential for profit. The invention of the cotton gin in the 1790s, coupled with the free labor of thousands of enslaved people, translated into incredible riches for early white settlers. Between 1798, when Mississippi became a US territory, and 1817, when it became a state, the population of Europeans and enslaved people in northern Mississippi exploded.

Soon the Chickasaw were vastly outnumbered and out-resourced. Gradually, through a series of "treaties," they were forcibly moved off their land and joined, with many other native peoples, the Trail of Tears to Oklahoma. This transforming, tragic event happened during the administration of President Andrew Jackson.

## Slavery

On land taken from the Chickasaw, white settlers began using the work of enslaved Africans to grow and harvest cotton. This combination of stolen land and forced labor propelled Mississippi to become the fourth richest state in the Union.[2]

The social, political, and economic foundations of Mississippi were built on slavery. This was nowhere clearer than in Mississippi's Declaration of Secession, which preceded the Civil War:

> Our position is thoroughly identified with the institution of slavery, the greatest material interest of the world.

When the Civil War ended and slavery was abolished, the state was in ruins. After Mississippi was readmitted to the Union, state authorities created five new counties, including Benton, to find jobs for local people and keep blacks and northerners from holding important positions in government. Benton was formed out of eastern Marshall and western Tippah counties in 1870. It is sometimes thought that Benton County was named in honor of Thomas Hart Benton, a senator from Missouri who fought against the expansion of slavery, but it was in fact named in honor of Colonel Samuel Benton, a Confederate veteran of the Civil War.

### Reconstruction

The decade following the Civil War, known as Reconstruction, saw stunning success and epic failure in Mississippi and throughout the South. Blacks were voting and holding office in substantial numbers for the first time. Over two hundred black Mississippians were elected to office during Reconstruction, including the first black United States senators: Hiram Rhodes Revels and Blanche K. Bruce.[3]

Benton County experienced this as well, and blacks participated in civic life in astounding new ways. In 1879, there were 1,282 white and 918 "colored" registered voters in Benton County. In three of Benton's most populated cities—Michigan City, Lamar, and Salem—black voters *outnumbered* white voters.[4] During this period, blacks ran for political office in Benton County as well. The *Ashland Register* in 1879 reported that A. J. Terry, a "colored" man, was a candidate for assessor, and is also described as the son of Solomon Terry, a member of the previous Board of Registrars.[5] Terry lost the assessor race by only two hundred votes.[6] This political power was not limited to the voting booth, but was present

Ancestors of Theris Roberston Rutherford. Courtesy of
Aviva Futorian.

in the courtroom as well. In 1879, a jury composed of eight "coloreds" and four
whites, voted to execute Robert Fox, a black man, for the murder of Harrison
Saxton, whose race was not reported.[7] While the specifics of that particular case
are unclear, the makeup of that jury is telling. In the first years after the Civil
War, blacks were registering to vote, organizing, holding office, buying land, and
participating in civic life. It would be almost one hundred years before another
black person ran for office or was seated on a jury in Benton County.

### The Rise of Jim Crow

Shortly after re-entry into the Union, with its economy in shambles, the Mississippi State Legislature passed what came to be known as "Black Codes." This
legislation intended to continue the institution of slavery under a different name.
Restrictions on formerly enslaved people (also called "freedmen") to voting,
bearing arms, using public transportation, renting land, and assembling were
written into law. Blacks who wanted to register to vote now had to pass literacy
tests. The Codes, which later became known as Jim Crow, were statutes that
physically segregated people by race, and legally discriminated against blacks
in all aspects of their lives.[8]

### Sharecropping and Landownership

Only a few formerly enslaved people were able to save enough money and find
a willing white landowner who would sell them land. In these conditions, the

practice of sharecropping was born. Spence Richard, a sharecropper and civil rights activist who appears in chapter 2, described the practice:

> The man fronted [the land and] the mule. He fed us. Bought us clothes. And he got half of the crop we made. If we made ten bales, he got five. And then he'd take any expenses out of our half and then if we had anything left, he would give us that. He got his part, you might say, clear. But we paid for our part outta what we made. Sometimes we cleared somethin', and sometimes we didn't.

The majority of blacks in Benton County were sharecroppers when the county was formed in 1870. Despite various legal, financial, and social obstacles, some black people owned land at the time. They also bought or acquired land throughout the nineteenth and twentieth centuries, even though many were later swindled or even killed for their land by whites.[9]

## Education

Public education for blacks did not exist prior to Benton County's formation. In 1870, the Mississippi Reconstruction Legislature established a public school system for everyone in the State. By 1890, this mandate was replaced by Jim Crow, which remained in effect for black people for over seventy-five years: strict control over the curriculum, dangerously rundown facilities, low salaries for teachers, and poor, second-hand resources.

Cotton-producing counties, such as Benton, adapted their black school calendars to the cotton crop needs, turning out in the early spring, "choppin' time." School resumed in the broiling summer months and turned out again in September and October, "pickin' time." It was a schedule that reflected the priorities of the white power structure. When it came to black people, manual labor was more important than education.

Between 1865 and 1936, black citizens in Benton County built several one-room schoolhouses on land donated by black landowners, and they petitioned the county board of education to permit their establishment and pay their teachers.[10]

Many counties, including Benton, did not have high schools for blacks until the 1940s.[11] Most early black schools were in churches. Sometime in the 1940s, Mose Terry, a black landowner in Benton County, sold an acre of land to the county to build a one-room schoolhouse, called Old Salem. It was black residents themselves who obtained surplus federal lumber and built this school (and others) for their children.

Unknown class of Harris Chapel school students. Courtesy of the Benton County Historical Society.

The faculty dormitory of the original Old Salem school.

Black schools in Benton County had an average daily attendance of between twelve and sixty-six students, and several grades were taught at once. Except for a very brief period at the beginning of Reconstruction, the teachers were black and studied at colleges established by the black communities.[12]

In 1954, the US Supreme Court issued the landmark decision *Brown v. Board of Education*. The court ruled unanimously that racial segregation in public schools was unconstitutional. The decision rejected the notion of legal segregation and directed states to end it with "all deliberate speed." Lacking a firm deadline, Mississippi and other states were slow to adopt the ruling.

In 1958, the Benton County government built the Old Salem School (named after the original, which was built exclusively by the black community) for black

1960 Old Salem Attendance Center yearbook photo. Courtesy of the Benton County Historical Society.

students. This was an attempt to avoid desegregation by giving the appearance of "equal" facilities. Four years after *Brown* rejected the concept of separate but equal, the county was still beginning to cling to it.

## Racial Violence

Violence had been an integral part of the system of slavery, and the threat of it was ever present during Reconstruction and thereafter. The Ku Klux Klan was established in 1871 in Pulaski, Tennessee, just over two hours from Benton County.

The first documented lynching in Benton County is reported in the *Southern Advocate* in 1923: a black man, charged with killing a white man, was taken from jail by an armed white mob and hung from a tree. The paper reported:

> This is the first lynching that has taken place in Benton County since the organiza-
> tion of the county. . . . The mob was very quiet and orderly in its procedure, and
> there was no marks or evidence to show that the Negro was abused, beaten or tor-
> tured in any way. He was hanged by the neck and one shot fired through his body.

Other lynchings were documented, as well as some that appear repeatedly in the memories of interviewees:

- Between 1920 and 1930, John Henry Remmer, a black man, was accused of killing a white man on Highway 5 over an argument. Remmer was arrested and taken to the jail in Ashland, where he was intercepted by a white mob and lynched.
- In 1923, Oliver Maxey, who was half-white, was a merchant and land-owner who donated land for New Hope School on his farm and was a teacher in it. He had a store on what is now Highway 72. He was killed by a white mob and his store burned down.
- The Pamm brothers were accused of running whiskey in Grand Junction, Tennessee. They were caught and killed, but first they killed several whites. The remaining Pamm family members, who owned land, fled to Memphis, leaving the land to be taken by whites.[13]
- In 1933, two black men from Benton County, Robert "Isey" Jones and Smith Houey, were lynched for allegedly killing a white man and burning down his store. Jones was also accused of killing an officer. A white mob hung them from a tree on Meridian Road near Michigan City. The next day, their bodies were displayed on the ground with ropes still around their necks for all who passed by to see.[14]
- Pete Harris was a black man who came to Benton County in the 1940s to work with a white female traveling nurse at the Ashland clinic. He would often drive her around to make home visits, causing many hostile comments. His body was found in a pond west of the fairgrounds in Ashland, in the back of Clyde Hudspeth's house.

Outside of Benton County, three instances of racial violence in Mississippi received an enormous amount of press and loomed large in the memories of several interviewees: the mutilation and murder of Emmett Till in Tallahatchie County in 1955; the assassination of civil rights leader Medgar Evers in Jackson in 1963; and in the summer of 1964, the murder of civil rights workers James Chaney, Andrew Goodman, and Michael Schwerner in Neshoba County.

### Henry Reaves and the Formation of the Citizens Club

Despite the many obstacles facing them, between 1902 and 1937, 109 blacks (including two women) managed to register to vote in Benton County.[15] Black

Henry Reaves, 1920s. Courtesy of the
Reaves family.

Henry Reaves in his pickup truck. Courtesy of Frank Cieciorka.

registration was not limited to those who owned land, as long as the registrant
could pay a poll tax and a white man "vouched" for him. One of the indications
of this was that many black registrants listed other people as their employers,
likely whites on whose land they were sharecropping.

Henry Reaves (b. 1900), to whom this book is dedicated, was a farmer, landowner, and the leading civil rights organizer in the county. As early as the late

Benton County local people at a civil rights meeting. Courtesy of Frank Cieciorka.

1920s, he attended NAACP meetings in Mound Bayou and elsewhere in the state. During World War II, he initiated a civil rights group in Benton County called the Citizens Club, an organization that would be the heart of the movement in the county. They met secretly at Greenwood and Macedonia churches, and focused on voter registration. They also raised money for NAACP lawyers to bring voter registration and other antidiscrimination lawsuits against the state. Participants included Walter and Annie Mae Webber, Sarah and Joe Washington, Jessie and Kenny Crawford, Mabel Traylor, Sarah Robinson, Robert Lee Bean, and Loyal and Thelma Thompson.

### Freedom Summer and Beyond

In June 1964, white civil rights volunteers from the North came to Mississippi. They were trained and organized by the Student Nonviolent Coordinating Committee (SNCC), one of the major activist civil rights organizations in the country in the early 1960s. SNCC was among three groups working in Mississippi under the umbrella of the Council of Federated Organizations (COFO).

SNCC volunteers, led by Ivanhoe Donaldson and Stokely Carmichael (later known as Kwame Ture), contacted Henry Reaves in Benton County. The purpose of the volunteers' presence was not to organize local people. Rather, SNCC organizers believed that the presence of white students from the North would focus the nation's attention on the segregation, inequality, and violence that local blacks were living under, and would thus make local black people safer in their organizing efforts. The project became known as Freedom Summer. These volunteers undertook several initiatives, working under the direction of Reaves and the Benton County Citizens Club.[16]

Black people in the county were very receptive to the civil rights workers, mainly because Mr. Reaves had spent years laying the groundwork. During the years before 1964, Reaves spent a good deal of time talking with Benton County congregations about voting. Once volunteers arrived and the need for larger meetings became clear, the vast majority of black churches agreed, at great risk, to host civil rights meetings: Greenwood, Hardaway, Harris, Hebron, Macedonia, Mount Zion CME, Palestine, Samuel's Chapel, Sims, Sand Hill, and Union Hill. The Citizens Club focused on voter registration, equal treatment by the government in agricultural programs, improving the black school, and preparing for school desegregation.

People from all over the country provided support for the civil rights movement in Mississippi. For example, Milton Herst, who owned a fabric shop in Chicago, sent huge barrels of fabric scraps to Benton County. Women in the county made beautiful patch quilts, some of which were sold at a SNCC outlet in New York called Liberty House, which was run by the counterculture activist Abbie Hoffman.

## Freedom Schools

In addition to these initiatives, "Freedom Schools" were established in 1964. The schools, held at Mount Zion Church and Harris Chapel and taught by local residents and SNCC volunteers, focused on reading and critical thinking. Taught by local residents and SNCC volunteers, Freedom Schools focused on stimulating students' interest in learning and on developing their sense of self-worth and self-confidence. Perhaps most important, the Freedom Schools taught students how to ask questions, which they had learned not to do in order to protect themselves in a racist society.

In the fall of 1964, at the end of the summer project, many volunteers headed back north. Aviva Futorian, a SNCC volunteer from the North,[17] stayed as the outside civil rights organizer in Benton County. She was supported at ten dollars a week by a Friends of SNCC chapter in Boulder, Colorado. Also working in the county were local resident James Batts, and volunteers Frank Cieciorka, Robert Smith, and Bob Traer. During the winter of 1964–65, Cieciorka and Futorian held a college prep class once a week during the evening at the home of Howard and Annie Evans. Students were Clay and Laura Batts,[18] Ernestine and Janeival Evans, Alberta Tipler, George "Dewey" Washington, Roy Nunnally, and Roy DeBerry (of Marshall County). Every one of these students went

Freedom School students
outside Mount Zion Church.
Courtesy of Frank Cieciorka.

Alberta Tipler. Courtesy of Frank
Cieciorka.

Roy Nunnaly graduation portrait. Courtesy of
the Benton County Historical Society.

Jenevial Evans. Courtesy of Aviva Futorian.

Ernestine Evans. Courtesy of Frank Cieciorka.

Roy DeBerry. Courtesy of Roy DeBerry.

George Dewey Washington. Courtesy of Frank Cieciorka.

Clay Batts. Courtesy of the Batts family.

to college: DeBerry to Brandeis on scholarship; Clay Batts and Tipler to the University of Wisconsin on scholarship.

Freedom Schools were also conducted in the summer of 1965. That fall, Aviva Futorian left Benton County and local resident Alberta Tipler became the full-time civil rights organizer. For a few weeks, she was assisted by Don Jelinek, a volunteer lawyer from New York.

### The *Benton County Freedom Train*

Beginning in June 1964 and lasting consistently for two years (and sporadically for two more), the Citizens Club put out a mimeographed newsletter called the *Benton County Freedom Train*. The *Freedom Train* had news, stories, essays, and poems about black empowerment and freedom written by Benton County residents, many of them young people. Someone in the North raised money to send a mimeograph machine to Benton County, which created an efficient means to produce many copies.

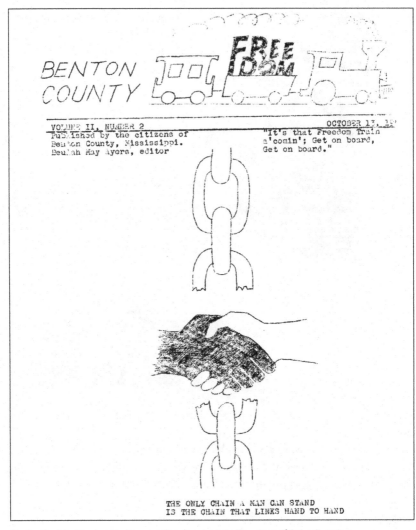

*Benton County Freedom Train* cover, October 13, 1964. Courtesy of Aviva Futorian.

Beulah Mae Ayers was the editor, and dozens of people were active in writing for and distributing the newspaper. As the movement gained momentum, the need for a space of its own became evident. In July of 1965, the Citizens Club erected its own office on land belonging to Carey Tipler (the father of Albert Tipler, who's featured in chapter 2). The paper was mimeographed in the Citizens Club office and distributed clandestinely by car and hand delivered throughout the county. Whenever a civil rights worker's car passed by, share-croppers working white people's land would run out of the fields to grab a pile of *Freedom Trains*. Walter Reaves, one of the Citizens Club section leaders, said:

*Benton County Freedom Train* cover, October 20, 1964. Courtesy of Aviva Futorian.

I'd take so many and distribute them out to different people—whoever was interested in it. I'd offer it to 'em whether they wanted it or not. The most of them always took the *Freedom Train.*

Possession of the newsletter was dangerous for black people, especially sharecroppers. It indicated an involvement with "outside agitators," as civil rights volunteers were known, and risked eviction or worse. Since the mainstream papers refused to carry civil rights news,[19] the *Freedom Train* might have been the only record in north Mississippi of the events of these times.[20]

Beulah Mae Ayers, editor of the *Benton County Freedom Train*. Courtesy of Frank Cieciorka.

Roy Nunnally operating the Benton County Freedom Train mimeograph machine. Courtesy of Frank Cieciorka.

Community members building the Citizens Club Office. Courtesy of Aviva Futorian.

Community members building the Citizens Club Office. Courtesy of
Aviva Futorian.

The Benton County Citizens Club office, completed in July 1965.
Courtesy of Aviva Futorian.

*Benton County Freedom Train* cover, July 11, 1965. Courtesy of Aviva Futorian.

## Voter Registration

The 1890 Mississippi Constitution required all persons registering to vote to pay a poll tax for two years prior to registering, and interpret a section of the Mississippi Constitution to the satisfaction of the county registrar. This created an economic, social, and legal barrier for blacks to register. In the early 1960s, many black Benton County citizens attempted to register but were turned down

9/17/64

CARD OF THANKS
'e would like to thank our
nds and neighbors for all the
dness shown to us in the death
d, flowers and kind words —
' God bless you,
G. W. Russum and children.

FOR RENT

R RENT NOW—The F.H.A. of-
on south side of square in Ash-
d. Airconditioned, with com-
de. and wash basin. I'll rent as
Nice location for business. F.
Hudspeth.                    3t-10-1p

LOST AND FOUND

ST — Black and tan female
und near Jim Wilson's store.$10
information leading to her re-
very. A. N. Jones, Dumas, Miss.
one Ripley 7890.          2t-9-24p

ST AND DANGEROUS — One
ack angus bull, weighs about
00 lbs. Has ring in nose with
out two foot chain in it. Wallace
rown, Grand Junction, Tenn, Rt.
                               9-24p

KEN UP—One whitefaced cow,
t my farm. Wallace Brown, Rt. 2
rand Junction, Tenn.       9-24p

SPECIAL NOTICES

O WHOM IT MAY CONCERN:
The following vehicle will be
old 4 weeks from this date to the
ighest bidder for settlement of
.recker and storage charges.
1938 Chevrolet 4-door sedan,
Bel-Air, Motor No. F38A129138.
This vehicle was abandoned 1
nile east of Winborn, Miss., on
ighway 78, approximately 8
nonths ago and stored since at
Davis Auto Parts, Hickory Flat,
Miss., now owned by R. H. Scott.
                               10-1p

STRAYED—One Duroc brood sow
with wire in nose. Left my home
Aug. 29th. Notify Clabon Jackson,
Michigan City, Miss. Near Harda-
way pond, for reward.    3t-9-24p
Michigan City,Miss. Near Harda-

POSTED—All land owned by me
in Benton County is posted against
hunting and all trespassing. George
L. Luna.                    9-1-64p

POSTED—All land owned and
controlled by me is posted against
hunting and trespassing. Mrs. J. W.
Hardaway, Michigan City, Miss.
                               6-63p

POSTED—All land owned by us
is posted against hunting and all

RELIEVES PAIN AS
IT DISSOLVES CORNS AWAY
Now remove corns the fast, easy way
with Freezone®. Liquid Freezone relieves pain instantly, works below the
skin line to dissolve corns away in just
days. Get Freezone...at all drug counters.

POSTED—All land owned and
controlled by me is posted against
hunting and trespassing and livestock running at large. H. J. Gurley.

POSTED

All land owned and controlled by
Oscar Oakley in Benton County,
Mississippi, is posted against hunt-
ing, fishing, timber cutting and
trespassing, also all leased lands.
This will be enforced.
        OSCAR OAKLEY, Owner
        BOB HARRISON, Mgr.

NOTICE
All land owned or controlled
by C. B. Bright Sr., C. B.
Bright Jr., W. E. Bright, including McDonald land, also all
of Lewellen Est. (400 acres)
plus 80 acres owned by Mack
Lewellen, is posted against all
kinds of trespassing, especially
against bird hunting. Rider on
duty. Please take warning. L.
W. Miles.               11-28-64p

INSURANCE PROTECTION –

We Are Authorized Agents For –

U.S.F. & G. Insurance Co. — Home Insurance
Co. — Western Casualty Surety Co. — Boston
Insurance Co. — Citizens Insurance Co.
United States Fire Insurance Co.

And Will Write All Types of Insurance for
You Including;

Fire and Storm on your home, Collision
Insurance on your Vehicles, and all Types of
Liability Insurance

ASHLAND INSURANCE AGENCY
Niles Autry        -:-        W. B. Gresham
    Phone 4321              Ashland, Miss.

jection to any assessment thereon
contained, may file the same in
writing, on or before September
29, 1964, at 7:00 o'clock P.M., and
the Board will convene shortly
thereafter and will consider said
objections and remain in session
from day to day until all such
objections have been heard and
action taken thereon.
    Witness my signature, on this
the 1st day of September, 1964.
        s/D. G. BAKER
        Town Clerk
        (TOWN SEAL)

SWORN WRITTEN APPLICATION
FOR REGISTRATION TO VOTE
   Tommy Eldrich Williams, Michi-
gan City, Miss.  Henry White,
Holly Springs, Miss. Clee Anna
Tipler, Holly Springs, Miss. Onie
Lee Williams, Moscow, Tenn.
Robert Dale Aslinger, Ashland,
Miss. Jeff Alexander, Holly
Springs, Miss. Burne L. Alexander,
Holly Springs, Miss. Sarah Frances
Rutherford, Holly Springs, Miss.
Arthur Taylor Jeffries, Lamar,
Miss. Lola Mae Crenshaw, Potts
Camp, Miss.

SWORN WRITTEN APPLICATION
FOR REGISTRATION TO VOTE
   Curtis Epps, Michigan City, Miss.
Sarah E. Robinson, Michigan City,
Miss. Lucille G. Duncan, Michigan
City, Miss. Bobie Louise Harris,
Miss.

SWORN WRITTEN APPLICATION
FOR REGISTRATION TO VOTE
   Aaron Jones, Michigan City, Miss.
James Larry Childers, Ashland,
Miss.

lieves pains of tired, sore f...
STANBACK acts fast yet so
tly, and with pain relieved
feel relaxed, comfortable.
STANBACK's combination for:
free you from pain due to over
ercise and other muscular ach
STANBACK Tablets or Pow

REWARD
FOR INFORMATION AND :
of persons (wrongdoers) k
whereabouts of missing li
belonging to me; willfully
ing fencing or trees; re
posted signs; shooting at liv
or running livestock of an
Shoup family since 1878, 1
1954). Strictly no hun
trespassing is permitted.
          SHOUP     RAN
MAJOR SAMUEL E. SH

COLD SUFFERE
Get fast relief from that a
over, worn-out feeling due t:
STANBACK's combination o
cally-proven ingredients r
fever and brings comforting
Use as a gargle for sore throa
colds. Snap back with STAN

Bring your Films to
                for Developing
Good Work        Quick
CHAPMAN-GRAY DRUG
Ashland       West side o

SAVE
4%
DIVIDEND ON
PASS BOOK
DEPOSITS.

NORTH MISS
Sunflower Center
NEW ALBANY, MIS:
Phone 534-4336

List of names in the *Southern Advocate*, September 17, 1964. Courtesy of Aviva Futorian.

because they "failed" to interpret sections of the Mississippi Constitution to
the "satisfaction" of Lawson Mathis, the county registrar. In addition to these
hurdles, intimidation (including the publication of registrants' names in the
local paper, the *Southern Advocate*), harassment, and eviction of sharecroppers
who tried to vote were commonplace. Despite these challenges, many black
people made several attempts to register. Perhaps chief among them was Burne
Alexander, a Benton County activist and poet, who attempted at least *thirteen
times* before succeeding. Her name was constantly in the paper.

By the beginning of Freedom Summer, the official Mississippi Democratic
Party disallowed participation for nonwhites. This rendered Mississippi's 40

Burne Alexander. Courtesy of Frank Cieciorka.

The Mississippi Freedom Democratic Party. Courtesy of Roy DeBerry.

The Reverend John Henry "Lightnin'" Beard. Courtesy of Frank Cieciorka.

percent black population without any political power. To counter this, SNCC, working with local people, developed an alternative party—the Mississippi Freedom Democratic Party (MFDP)—to challenge and desegregate the state party. The party was cofounded by a sharecropper and activist from Sunflower County named Fannie Lou Hamer. In August 1964, MFDP sent representatives, including Henry Reaves, to the Democratic National Convention in Atlantic City. The goal was to be recognized as the state's official delegation. While that goal fell short, the effort led to increased national attention on the lack of voting rights and political power for blacks in Mississippi.[21]

On December 1, 1964, the US Justice Department brought the Benton County registrar to trial in federal court in Oxford. Scores of black residents provided documents and testimony proving the Benton County registrar engaged in voter harassment and intimidation. Just before the trial was to begin, officials from Benton County offered to try to work out an agreement with the Justice Department. The result was a temporary settlement whereby the voter rolls were wiped clean and the registrar's office was closed, pending a final agreement.

Benton County's voter registration office was reopened five months later in May 1965 with the expectation that over 90 percent of black registrants would be accepted. Within the first month, only 60 percent of the 240 blacks who attempted to register were accepted. Lawson Mathis, the registrar, would not

L. B. Paige. Courtesy of Frank Cieciorka.

Sarah Robinson at a meeting. Courtesy of Frank Cieciorka.

take printing or "bad" handwriting, would not tell blacks why they "failed," and did not give blacks a chance to correct their mistakes. As a result, the US Justice Department obtained a court order permitting people to register to vote without paying poll tax or interpreting the Constitution.

In August 1965, the federal Voting Rights Act took effect. Among other provisions, the act mandated that federal registrars take over local offices if local registrars refused to register black applicants. Between the large numbers of blacks attempting to register, and the refusal of Lawson Mathis to register them, on September 25, 1965, Benton County became the fifth (and smallest) Mississippi county to have a federal registrar appointed. The Reverend and Mrs. John Henry Beard were the first to register. Within one month, more than seven hundred blacks became registered voters in Benton County. By the end of 1965, about one thousand blacks were registered to vote, one of the highest black voter registration rates in the state.

## Holding Office

In addition to registering voters, the Citizens Club was looking for blacks to obtain political office as well. One of the targeted areas for this was agricultural committees. Federal law provided several agricultural programs, including cotton allotments, financial subsidies, and FHA loans, that were intended to benefit small landowners and sharecroppers or renters looking to purchase land. The distribution of these benefits, however, was handled by local agricultural committees. In Benton County, no black had ever served on one or had even been nominated. That changed in November of 1964, when the Citizens Club filed nominating papers for eight black candidates. Crucially, anyone who worked the land could vote in these elections, whether they owned land or not. At the request of the Citizens Club, federal agents were present at the counting of the ballots. Three of the eight black candidates won election to an agricultural committee: L. B. Paige, Sarah Robinson, and Clabon Jackson. This was the first time since Reconstruction that blacks were elected to public office in Benton County.

## The Old Salem Boycott

More than ten years after *Brown v. Board of Education*, Mississippi was still segregating school children, and Benton County was no different. Ashland was the white-only school, and Old Salem was for blacks. The schools were far from

Roy Williamson. Courtesy of Frank Cieciorka.

equal in terms of facilities, books, class size, teacher pay, and leadership. The principal of Old Salem was a black man named W. B. "Woody" Foster, who was installed by the all-white school board and answered to them. Frustrated at the low quality of education, Citizens Club members went to see him on several occasions to try to get him to improve conditions in the school. He ignored them.

Tensions between Foster and the Citizens Club boiled over in January 1965. Old Salem hosted a high school basketball game, and SNCC organizer Aviva Futorian attended. Shortly after arriving, Foster told her that the superintendent had instructed him to tell her to leave. When she and the students she was sitting with refused, the county sheriff was brought in. In full view of all the students attending the game, she was arrested, placed in the sheriff's car, and driven away. News of the arrest and Foster's role in it spread fast. Students, getting off their school buses that day, told their families, who told other families. According to the *Freedom Train*, during the several hours Futorian was detained, Benton County residents surrounded the jail, and the bail (set at $1,000) was made by local black landowners Jeff Alexander, Roy Williamson, and Joe King.

On February 1, 1965, a delegation of black parents went to the white county school board, presented a report on the substandard conditions at Old Salem, and asked that Foster be replaced by the vice-principal, Lloyd Peterson, a Benton county native (which Foster was not). They also had several other requests for strengthening the educational program at Old Salem, such as establishing a

Henry Reaves, center, at the March 16, 1965, Citizens Club meeting voting to boycott Old Salem. Courtesy of Frank Cieciorka.

library and hiring a librarian. The school board met again twice with the Citizens Club before offering a deal: it would fire Foster and let blacks run "their" school if the Citizens Club would agree to not integrate Ashland School. The Citizens Club refused and on March 9, 1965, voted to boycott Old Salem. The very next day, only 130 black students attended, while 1,070 boycotted.

During the school boycott, five Freedom Schools were set up on the model of the previous summer.[22] The Freedom Schools were managed by the students from Frank Cieciorka and Aviva Futorian's college prep class, and taught by volunteers from Rust College. They were held in poorly heated, one-room wooden churches,[23] where students were cold but well fed by enthusiastic parents. The spirit of the Freedom Schools was resurrected, and students like Walter Lee Poplar were very engaged:

> I love Freedom School. It makes me feel like a new boy. I feel like I can speak for my rights.[24]

The few sharecroppers in the county did not fare so well, however. Billy Carpenter, a white landowner, demanded that Buck Nelson, who was a sharecropper on Carpenter's land, send his children to school. When Nelson refused, Carpenter immediately evicted Nelson from his property. More than fifty years later, the children of Buck Nelson, who appear in chapter 3, still had memories of spending a cold, rainy night in a leaky barn.

*Benton County Freedom Train* cover, January 17, 1965. Courtesy of Aviva Futorian.

The boycott of Old Salem had other effects, as well. Some of the bus drivers began supporting the boycott by bringing students in their own vehicles to Freedom Schools, an act that got them fired. On the day they were fired, the bus drivers left work[25] and along with Citizens Club section captain Walter Reaves, integrated the all-white Ashland Café, on the northeast corner of Ripley and Court in Courthouse Square.

They were not, however, the first to do so. A few weeks before, two groups of black women seized the momentum the movement was gaining. When a new textile factory opened in Ashland, these women spent two days apply-

*Benton County Freedom Train* cover, January 24, 1965. Courtesy of Aviva Futorian.

ing for jobs at a new shirt factory in Ashland. In between applications, they entered the Ashland Café and J. K. Percell's Café, which until then were all-white establishments. They were treated courteously and served, but the County Attorney Tony Farese came to the café and demanded to know each of their names. The sheriff trailed their car out of town.[26] Shortly after this, Aubrey Bean integrated the Cotton Patch Café, as did Fred Richard Jr., who was arrested, allegedly for an "improper muffler," and taken to jail until he got someone to pay a fine of twenty dollars, for which the Citizens Club reimbursed him.

Meanwhile, the boycott of Old Salem continued. By the end of March 1965, the county was losing state money because of the lowered student enrollment, and the school board gave in. On April 5, 1965, Woody Foster submitted his letter of resignation and was replaced by Benton County native Lloyd Peterson.

The repercussions were swift, however. At least six black teachers who were supportive of the Citizens Club did not have their contracts renewed. Foster, under the encouragement of John Farese, a white Benton County lawyer, sued ten leaders of the Citizens Club, along with Aviva Futorian, for libel. Pointing to *Freedom Train* issues that called Foster a "puppet," "dummy," and "Uncle Tom," he sought $600,000 in damages. It was an attempt to shut the Citizens Club and the movement down. The trial was held in August 1965. Representing the defendants were volunteer lawyers from the Lawyers' Constitutional Defense Committee: Mark DeWolfe Howe, a renowned Harvard Law School professor,[27] and John Saltonstall, an eminent lawyer from Boston. Despite excellent representation, Judge Walter O'Barr awarded Foster $60,000. The Mississippi Supreme Court ultimately reversed O'Barr's decision (Reaves and Futorian et. al v. Foster) declaring that the Citizens Club had a right to publicly criticize the school system and its principal because he was a public figure. The Citizens Club owed no money. During the next judicial election cycle, Judge O'Barr sent letters to all the black voters in Benton County, asking to let bygones be bygones and re-elect him. The voters, now swelled with newly registered blacks, overwhelmingly voted him out of office.

### School Desegregation

Along with voting rights, school desegregation was the civil rights issue towards which the Citizens Club worked most passionately. It was also the issue opposed by whites most vehemently.

In June 1965, 44 parents and 107 students filed suit against Benton County to desegregate its school system. They were represented by Henry Aronson of the NAACP Legal Defense and Education Fund.

In July 1965, the federal court ordered the Benton County School System to initiate a "Freedom of Choice" school desegregation plan. Benton County responded with a staggered system, allowing black children at certain grade levels to choose to attend the white school. In the first year of Benton County's desegregation, the plan applied to the first, tenth, eleventh, and twelfth grades; the following year, it applied to more grades, and so forth. Siblings were allowed to register in other grades.

Freedom of Choice put the onus on individual black families to enroll in all-white schools. Black parents who wanted their children to attend all-white schools had to step forward to register in a very conspicuous fashion. It was an incredibly risky decision for the student and the families, but many took that risk. The reasons were political and moral, but also deeply personal. Black families knew the white schools had superior facilities, programs, and books, and they simply wanted a better education for their children. Eugene Steward, who appears in chapter 2, told us,

> I made the decision for Bobbie. She had to go, 'cause I told her I didn't figure I should fight for something I didn't believe in myself. I know the books they was getting. When they was out of date, they would send them back to Old Salem. And I wanted my kids to have a good education. A better education than they were getting.

Black students suffered countless insults: being spat on, forced to get off the sidewalk, ridiculed for misspelling a word, hit by flying objects, and other petty slights by classmates. Racial epithets were commonplace. Some of the students recalled singular, major incidents that became seared in their memory; others remembered countless daily indignities.

### Violent Reaction

Following clear victories like school desegregation and increased black voter registration, white extremists responded with violence, beginning in the fall of 1965. Car tires were slashed in school parking lots, crosses were burned in the yards of black families, dead animals were left on their doorsteps, shots were fired at their houses, and people were trailed in their cars along the highway.

Three churches were burned in Benton County during the summer of 1965: Sanctified Church of God in Christ, Davis Temple, and Everetts Chapel. None of these churches had hosted civil rights meetings, but the first two were located off Highway 72 and therefore accessible to "night riders," caravans of Klansmen who would ride with guns at night, terrorizing black citizens. In August 1965, crosses were burned in front of the Citizens Club office, in front of civil rights activists' homes, and in front of the home of the white school superintendent. KKK rallies were held at the fairgrounds.

In October, there was an attempt to burn down the Citizens Club office, which had been built only a few months earlier. Cars and pickup trucks began driving through black neighborhoods, honking horns and firing shots. The FBI had agents in the area, who began chasing the perpetrators. Almost incredibly, two black men—Loyal Thompson and Jake Nunnally—joined the chase, ran the whites away and returned to put out the fire and save the Citizens Club office.

Jake Nunnally with his child.
Courtesy of Aviva Futorian.

Loyal Thompson at a Citizens Club meeting.
Courtesy of Aviva Futorian.

Ashland High School today. Courtesy of John Lyons.

Eldora Johnson, a resident of that neighborhood who appears in chapter 5, described Thompson and Nunnally as, "'bout the two bravest black men here."

## Resegregation

The last year of Freedom of Choice was 1970. As more blacks enrolled at Ashland, more whites left. At first, many left for Gray Academy, a private "Christian" school that did not have to abide by federal civil rights guidelines. These private academies sprung up all over the South after desegregation, so much so that they became known as "segregation academies." White students from Ashland had another avenue, however. There was one all-white school on the far southern part of the county, Hickory Flat.[28]

The result has been almost total resegregation of Benton County Schools, but with significant differences. The black schools get new books and equipment, facilities are relatively similar, and black students get a better education than forty years ago.

In 2008, the county's first black superintendent of education was elected after scandal and corruption brought down his predecessor. However, he served one term before being voted out in favor of a white superintendent. There have been a number of black school board members. While there has been improvement, a de facto segregated education system still exists in Benton County. A poor county of this size would struggle to support one campus adequately, let alone two. But the idea of consolidating and building a central school has been met with strong social, economic, and political resistance by the white community.

◆  ◆  ◆

Benton County has witnessed enormous struggles and profound victories in its history. This historical context is meant as a framework to better understand the stories in the pages that follow. This historical context is an abbreviated and imperfect history of a group and a place; the real heart of this book is the individual stories of people living in these times. The black citizens of Benton County recognized a need for change, and some of the poorest, most vulnerable people in America went about making it happen. After centuries of slavery, brutality, lynchings, discrimination, and injustice, they did it with clarity, purpose, and grace. As Crystal Steward says in chapter 2, paraphrasing a common sentiment:

It was all worth it. . . . We're not where we ought to be, but thank the Lord we're not where we used to be.

# Benton County

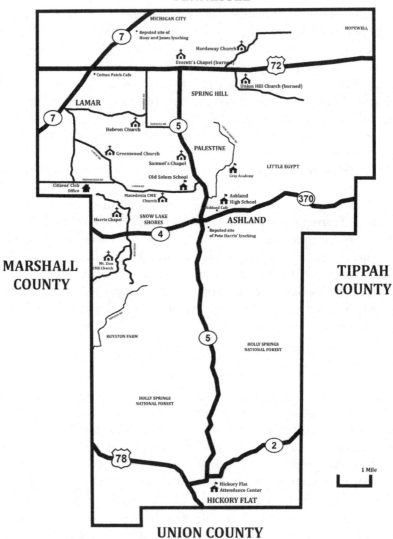

**TENNESSEE**

MICHIGAN CITY

HOPEWELL

⑦ * Reputed site of
Huey and Jones lynching

Hardaway Church

Everett's Chapel (burned)

⑦²

* Cotton Patch Cafe

Union Hill Church (burned)

SPRING HILL

**LAMAR**

⑦

Hebron Church

⑤

**PALESTINE**

LITTLE EGYPT

Greenwood Church

Samuel's Chapel

Old Salem School

Gray Academy

Citizens' Club
Office

Macedonia CME
Church

Ashland
High School

Harris Chapel

SNOW LAKE
SHORES

Ashland Cafe

**ASHLAND**

370

④

* Reputed site
of Pete Harris' lynching

**MARSHALL
COUNTY**

Mt. Zion
CME Church

**TIPPAH
COUNTY**

ROYSTON FARM

⑤

HOLLY SPRINGS
NATIONAL FOREST

HOLLY SPRINGS
NATIONAL FOREST

②

1 Mile

78

Hickory Flat
Attendance Center

**HICKORY FLAT**

**UNION COUNTY**

Benton County detail map. Courtesy of John Lyons.

# Voices from the Mississippi Hill Country

## Chapter 1

# BEGINNINGS

*The early years of the twentieth century in Benton County were a particularly difficult time for black residents. The specter of Jim Crow, a series of laws that mandated segregation, loomed large. Lynching was a constant threat. Sharecropping, the system of white landowners renting land to black residents for payment in crops, drove blacks deeper into debt and made them more dependent. Blacks were faced with numerous hurdles to vote, including a poll tax, a Constitution test, and openly bigoted registrars. Black schools had far fewer resources than white schools. Work was hard, the days very long, and prospects for a better future were dim. But in the following people are found the beginnings of Benton County's civil rights movement.*

# Sarah Robinson

## 1916–2008

Interviewed November 2004, Michigan City, Mississippi, by Aviva Futorian and John Lyons

*Ms. Robinson was a founding member of the Benton County Citizens Club and a section captain in the Michigan City chapter. Though born in Benton County, she was raised in Tennessee, where she worked as a sharecropper, among other jobs. She returned to Benton County as a young woman, worked for a period in Arkansas and Memphis, Tennessee, and came back for good in 1959, eventually inheriting land from her father. She was very active in Benton County, particularly around the issue of voting and distributing the movement's* Freedom Train *newspaper. "Oh, honey," she told us. "I gave 'em to everybody." She welcomed us into her home, and we had the following conversation in her living room.*

◆ ◆ ◆

My mother passed away in 1920, I understand, and a first cousin wanted a child. So my daddy let her have me. I grew up in Fayette County, Tennessee. I returned to Benton County in '34, I believe. I had grew up and got to be eighteen years old. It was what I thought to be a mean lady that reared me and I decided that I wasn't going to take no more whippins, and I decided to come back to Benton County and stayed with my brother and sister-in-law. We day-worked.

**Interviewer:** *How did that work?*

[Laughs.] Poorly, honey, poorly. Poorly! I'm tellin' you! We had to get up early and we had to stay late. The men had to get up and be at the barn at 5:00 a.m. Field work, choppin' cotton, honey, till twelve. Come in and hurry up and eat dinner, if there was anything to eat, and then go on out again. It'd be just about dark when we come in from the field.

My husband and I sharecropped. We were credited for fifty cents a day. We didn't get no money. The government was givin' out commodities.[1] And when we lived over there on this man's place, Marvin Curtis, we was supposed to be getting commodities. Then one time, he carried them up in his truck and each one got his own. All the other times Curtis got the commodity and put it in the storeroom. And we had to buy it from him.

Oh, honey, it wasn't easy. But somehow or another, we made it. We made it through. And, in 1941 I left there, both me and my husband, and went to Arkansas and was workin' by the day there. It was better there than it was here. We got commissary. Back then you didn't get money. Money went to the boss. The boss man gave us food from the commissary.

**Interviewer:** *When you moved back to Benton County, you inherited your father's land?*

Our dad, yeah. I think it worked out very well. I didn't know how many acres we had 'cause we did it in strips. We had twenty acres down there, sixteen over there, five and one-eighth over here, and twelve down there.

**Interviewer:** *Where did your father get his land from?*

From his forefather. Our grandfather, he came from Sussex County, Virginia,[2] I believe, and his wife came from Dinwiddie County, Virginia. They were slaves. The land, the slave master gave it to him, I guess.

◆ ◆ ◆

**Interviewer:** *What first got you interested in civil rights?*

Oh child, that votin'. The *voting*. Henry Reaves, he would come to our church and then he would have meetings and we would meet at different churches. He would tell us, "It's good to be a citizen. Vote. So you can have some voice." And that got me to thinkin' about it. And I wanted to be a citizen. Yeah, I wanted to be a citizen. So I can be considered somebody!

[Sighs.] Lawson Mathis.[3] We had to go to Oxford a time or two on him, you know. His friends and his colleagues, they would come down the hall yellin'. And we'd look up at him, and he'd cut his eye at us. I didn't pass the first time, I don't know whether I passed the second time. But I *passed*.

Sarah Robinson, during a visit a few years after
our conversation. Courtesy of Aviva Futorian.

My first contact [with the 1964 summer volunteer civil rights workers], I was
hearin' about this Robert Moses.[4] He got people, young people from all over the
States, I believe. I don't know where they met at, but they tell me he got them
together and they talked. And he told them, you know, the consequences. What
could or would happen. Them three boys—Goodman, Chaney, and Schwerner.[5]
I remember their killin', that was a senseless killin'. But they was willin' to take
the chance. You know, they were just killin' for nothin'. For nothin'. You didn't
have to do somethin', you know, to get messed up or maimed, or beat up or
killed, you know? You didn't have to do very much to get killed.

**Interviewer:** *Did you ever think of pulling out of the movement?*

No! Being in it felt so *good*. I didn't think about pullin' out. Being in it was so good.
   I was kinda skittish, though. I didn't know if they were gonna throw a bomb,
or shoot in the window. I didn't know, but I just kept God in my heart and mind
'cause I'm a great believer in the Bible. Lucky and blessed we are to come out
alive, because so many of them were killed. So many were killed.
   It's better than it was back then, I can tell you that. A whole lot better. Just
the atmosphere. You have to watch them [white people] to make them do right.
Mr. Reaves, he said, "You have to watch them. You have to *make* them do right.
They ain't gonna do right on their own." That's what Mr. Henry Reaves said.
He was right, too.

# Jessie Mae Epps

## 1919–2019

Interviewed April 2007, Michigan City, Mississippi, by Aviva Futorian, Roy DeBerry, and John Lyons

*The granddaughter of enslaved people, the hardships of Ms. Epps's ancestors are emblematic of the effort by her family to make a better life for themselves in the hills of north Mississippi. Her family was able to secure a significant amount of land earlier, which gave her a sense of freedom and independence. Ms. Epps was very active in the movement. She attended most meetings and made many attempts to register to vote before succeeding in the 1960s. She was Sarah Robinson's sister, and the following conversation took place in her kitchen.*

◆ ◆ ◆

My grandfather was Edmund Moore and he came from Sussex County, Virginia. I don't know the year. It's on his tombstone. And he walked here, I believe he said it took him six months to get here. He was a slave. It was my understanding he got his land through his master. They said it was about six hundred acres, and it was distributed among his children when he died.

I've done it all. I plowed, I chopped, I picked cotton, I pulled corn, I hauled corn, and I hoed. It was rough. You got up early in the morning and you milked the cows. After you milked the cows you got ready and you moved to the field. And you worked until about eleven, eleven thirty and you came back to the house and you ate lunch. Then at about one you went back out to the fields and you worked until sundown or after sundown, at least. School terms were short for us during those days. We had about four months out of the year for the black children to go to school.[6] It was kind of split up because you got to school a while then you have the school closed down and you'd have to harvest the crop. Then you go back to school.

**Interviewer:** *What are your first memories of the difference between blacks and whites?*

Let me see, how can I put this. We weren't raised around white children. We weren't raised around any at all. And we went to an all-black school, and I didn't see any of the white children. There wasn't any in the community, I didn't go to school with any, wasn't seeing any in the church. So I just didn't see any white children.

I'll tell you the truth—my father didn't talk certain things around children. There's just certain things he just didn't bring up. If you heard anything about it, you heard it from someone else because we didn't have no television at that time. You had to hear it through the grapevine. I can remember when I was a girl, there were three black men hung over here on number 5 [Highway 5]. I can remember hearing the discussions that the sheriffs said they could never find out who done it. They could never find out, so they said. Well, it looked like to me that it was just a little strange. And I can remember a black man was found somewhere in a pond in the county, dead. And they said they never could find out who done it. And you know, it looked like to me that they could find out *something*.

◆ ◆ ◆

I wanted to register and I wanted to vote. My oldest brother, he was registered. At that time, I think you had to pay two dollars, four dollars. Somethin' you had to pay.[7] I went to register and they gave me a form to fill out. Civil rights hadn't begun, hadn't come in yet at that time. And I believe there was a man named Mathis in there, at that time. And he gave me a form to fill out. And I don't know if I failed on the form or what. I didn't feel good. So few blacks was registered. So few. One here, there, and yonder was registered at that time. But I didn't try anymore until later years in the civil rights movement, and I didn't have any trouble. I did finally register.

I thought it was nice for them [civil rights volunteers] to come in here. But they wasn't welcome among white people. The black people welcomed them with open arms, but they wasn't welcomed by the white people. And the churches began to burn: Everetts Chapel and Union Hill. I'll be honest and tell you the truth, I was a little afraid sometimes, depending on where the meeting was. It looked like the group was pushing forward and I didn't want to be a "Tom."[8]

So, if I could do anything to help the cause I sure wasn't going to hinder it. And so I went along. I wasn't upfront but I was a strong supporter.

**Interviewer:** *You didn't have that kind of fear?*

No, I didn't. I know it could have happened. I remember we had a meeting once, out here at our church. We didn't go to that one because we didn't have transportation at the time. We would have had to walk. We would have walked a public road a piece and we would have turned and then crossed a field to the church. But there were so many people passing that it was almost like a funeral procession that night. And we didn't go. I kind of hate that we missed it, but we didn't go. Because we would have had to walk, and we just didn't go.

**Interviewer:** *Would you do it again?*

Yes, I would. Let's see, how do I put this? There was nothing for blacks to do but to go to the field. You go to school, you go to field, you go to church, you go to Sunday school, that was it. I believe a lot of our people now are enjoying the fruits of what it produced. There's some peoples in their own houses today that wouldn't have been where they been. And some of them are sitting in offices now who probably would not have been in offices if it had not been for the civil rights movement.

# Sallie Kimbrough

## Born 1921

Interviewed September 2011 and 2012, Ashland, Mississippi, by Aviva Futorian, Roy DeBerry, and John Lyons

*Ms. Kimbrough was widowed at the age of twenty-three, leaving her to care for seven children. She managed to raise those children, become an active member of the movement, care for her ailing parents, and somehow find the resources to purchase fifty acres of land after her husband passed away. Her brother-in-law was Junior Kimbrough, perhaps the most famous blues musician of the Hill Country area, who played a lesser known style than the more popular blues from the Mississippi Delta. We visited her home twice, including a few months before the re-election of Barack Obama.*

◆ ◆ ◆

I went to school in a church, we didn't have too far to walk. That's the only way we got there, was walking. We never got any new books, all of them was with the backs off. And the same books every year. I started at six years old and I went until I got eighteen, all with the same books. My momma and daddy wouldn't let us go to school until we got through gathering our crops, and other people would sometimes help, and we helped other people too. It took months to gather all of our crop. We had a big crop: cotton, corn, soybeans, sweet potatoes, and garden, we had all of that.

My daddy's daddy owned land. But Daddy just didn't pay the taxes on it. He owned acres of land he got from his daddy. Daddy didn't have the money and he didn't try, I reckon, to pay the taxes like he could. He let it go, and other peoples got it and sold it. I don't know who bought it. I know it was a white person.

My parents were sharecroppers. You worked and farmed and when you gathered the crop, it went to the peoples that own the land. You didn't never see nothing when you got through. It happens over and over, the same way. They raised cows and they'd get milk, hogs for meat, sorghum, molasses, and that's what we had to eat. We never had money to go to stores and shop. Mother and them, what little they got, they bought us clothes. They bought two dresses to go to school. When you pull one off and wash it, you put the other one on. One pair of shoes, and sometimes you walk that sole off of under that shoe going to school. You had to tie it with wire and go on.

It was quite a bit of violence here in Ashland before civil rights come in. I heard my daddy talk about the two boys who were lynched and hung from the tree in front of the courthouse.[9] They shot those boys. Daddy showed me what tree they were hanging in on Meridian Road. And that rope stayed up in them trees a long time. He told me how they shot them, cut them down, and let them fall on the ground like hogs. And carried them up there and laid them in the courtyard. I think some white lady accused them of winking at her or something like that.

We were just afraid. We never was around white people. Maybe some of them when we be picking cotton or something. We didn't go to no store, we wouldn't never have no money to go and shop in there. When we did, my momma sent us to fetch eggs and some fried chicken, and she sent us to the store to the get little things. And we went to the store and got that and just come right back. It was some fear.

**Interviewer:** *Did you ever wonder why white people were so mean?*

Always.

◆  ◆  ◆

I was about twenty-three when I got married. We made a living farming, rented from white peoples. My husband got poisoned. Another person who owned the place poisoned him. They held an inquest after he died, and told me he was poisoned. I was quite young and I didn't try to get no lawyer. Didn't know how. And they didn't do anything about it. That was in '58, I believe. After I lost him, I had to be on my own, farming and everything. At least I know it strengthened me. I had seven children when my husband passed. I had to raise them children. My mom and dad had moved in the house with me and they was there for me, too. But it strengthened me so much after I had to be on my own.

Sallie Kimbrough with child. Courtesy of the Kimbrough family.

Henry Reaves came to the house a lot [in the 1950s], but I had a jealous husband, and I never did get in with civil rights until after he was dead. I went twice to try to register to vote, the second time they let me pass. They just said I had to come back, I didn't get it right. That's what they told me. I wanted to vote because I wanted to have a name, I wanted to be like the other peoples. Mr. Reaves encouraged us all to vote, and also the civil rights peoples encouraged us, and I was determined to. I remember when we would get those *Freedom Trains* every time we went down to this church, Mount Zion, and different places like that, Samuel's Chapel, churches on the back roads. We would never go to the churches that was on the front road, to keep them from knowing what we were doing. We went to these churches in the back.

I cooked in a kitchen[10] [The Kudzu Cafe] right there in Ashland in '65. And one day some black women come inside. They walked in the *front* door. They had to go to the back door. They didn't want them in there, but they walked in. They let them sit in there but they weren't satisfied with them in there. Sure weren't. It just scared me, got me shook up. One of them was my niece. My sister's daughter, Mattie Smith.

Sallie Kimbrough's father, Solon Brown. Courtesy of the Kimbrough family.

That lady that owned the café, she said that she hoped they would throw Martin Luther King in the river. She just didn't want them in that restaurant. You could tell by the way she was acting. But they [the black women] didn't say anything. Later, when they killed Martin Luther King, I lost it. I lost it. I didn't want to be around her after she had spoke that about Martin Luther King. After he got killed, sure didn't. I finally quit. She ask me to come back because I was the head cook, but I didn't go back.

I went down to Sardis, Mississippi, one Sunday to a meeting with Henry Reaves and some civil rights workers. It was about us living better and trying to make a better living for ourselves. And when I got back home, a neighbor told me they had rented my house out. I told my kids, "Look y'all. I'm tired of moving, breaking up everything I got. I ain't gonna rent no more. I want to quit being pushed around by these white folks." That's exactly what I told them, so I went looking for some land.

**Interviewer:** *Did anybody say to you, "Women don't buy land?"*

They didn't really. I went to several people trying to buy land, but nobody didn't tell me that. You know how I bought this land? I bought this land, this two acres, in '65. This land was cheap, this is black man's land. [Laughs.] I sold cows, mostly.

No one stays here but me. I had eight kids, I lost three. Gracie, my oldest daughter, got killed right up there. A white man ran into her and just bent the truck up on her, about two years ago I lost her. And my other baby had lung cancer. And the third child had kidney cancer.

◆  ◆  ◆

**Interviewer:** *You have family in Chicago. Did you ever think of moving north?*

I did. I wanted to get away from Mississippi. We wasn't treated good. Had to work so hard and get nothing behind it. I didn't move north because I had my mom and dad with me. They didn't stay with nobody but me. After my husband died, they quit farming for themselves. They moved in the house with me, and they stayed here until the both of them died. I never thought about it no more, after I had some land. I was satisfied and then I was blessed. Now I got somewhere around fifty acres. I was born down here and I love it down here. After I got my little house to myself where I wouldn't have to move, I just love it. It's nice down here. It's a lot better than before. We had it rough. We didn't do nothing but know the fields. That's all we knew about, the fields and the church. We didn't own a nickel or dime or nothing. When we go to them civil rights meetings, we didn't know if we going to make it home or not. It was dangerous out there. I was scared, but I went. I wanted my rights. I was fighting for my rights.

White people is good people, but some of them was taught so badly against us. They hate, there's a lot of hatred. I never did think I would see a black president. And I'm so proud of that black president, but they treat him like he's a dog.

I think that they're learning better. For one thing, we're all in this world together. So much that's happened. They're so much different than they used to be, Lord Jesus. Most of them. Now you find just one or two snotty ones. They are sweet and they speak to you. Some of them, I *make* them speak to me. They used to wouldn't speak to you for nothing. But now, they might say a word or two to you. Young people now, it's a lot better than these old people. Young people—they should be proud of the freedom workers, they should be proud of them because when I come on it was rough. When I come up, I wished it would have been some freedom workers come in.

**Interviewer:** *What gave you the courage to be in the movement?*

I don't know. I guess it's built up in me. I got it from my parents, I've learned just to go to church and serve the Lord. That's from them.

# Teaster and Frances Baird

## Born 1935 (Teaster) and 1939 (Frances)

Interviewed January 2004, Lamar, Mississippi, by Aviva Futorian, Roy DeBerry, and John Lyons

*Mr. and Mrs. Baird were both active in the movement, especially at Samuel's Chapel Baptist Church, where Mr. Baird is a deacon. They had several reasons to decline to become involved: Mr. Baird's father was afraid for his son and discouraged his activism. Mr. Baird had opportunities in other parts of the country after his time in the army, including a lucrative offer to be hired as a land surveyor in Benton County. The offer came, however, with the caveat of disavowing the movement, a common tactic used by the white power structure to keep black residents from organizing. Despite this, they were both instrumental in the movement. "I could not go against the movement," Mr. Baird told us, "because I knew of the sweat and the blood." We talked with them in their living room, adorned with photographs of their grandchildren and of Mr. Baird's time in the service.*

◆ ◆ ◆

**Teaster:** My first school was Samuel's Chapel. About a mile from here, it was a school that went from first through the eighth grade. All the children was in that room, and we had one teacher. I stayed cold during the winter. My father came out once and talked with the teacher about my feet, you know, was getting cold. And so she would let me sit up a while to the fire, and just rotate me around. But I still stayed cold all day practically. My sister is the one who really taught me. I went to school, but, you know, I didn't learn anything, hardly. It was so crowded.

Something that kind of stuck with me—you know, early in life. It was two white men, they were called Buddy and Paul Baggins. We were afraid of those men. They would patrol the highway in an open, long bed truck. Didn't have a cab on it, didn't have any doors on it, and I was told that this driver would have a shotgun between his legs as he would drive. And they would harass black peoples. They would stop them sometimes, pull up on the side of them, try to force them off the road, you know. And we would be scared to walk the roads because we were afraid of Buddy and Paul Baggins. I would be afraid sometimes for my father, how he would go up and down those highways.

**Frances:** We were sharecroppers, and once we finished our crops we had to go and help other people. And we went to this white family to help pick cotton. And they would serve us lunch, and their family would eat at the tables, and we had to go to the back, I guess the chicken yard or whatever in the back. They would serve our lunch back there. So I asked my mom, "They eat in the kitchen, why couldn't we?" She said, "Well, that's just the way it is." And so that's just the way she explained it to us, "That's the way it is." And that's when I realized that there was a difference.

**Teaster:** My mother kind of overprotected us. She was a real religious person, and to help absolve some of the pain, would refer to us that we would overcome this when we get to heaven. We wouldn't understand why we had to go through so much. I learned to read real early. My father took the *Memphis Commercial Appeal*[11] and we started by reading the funnies. But what I'm getting down to is it was common to read about lynching black people. And they told us when they had these lynchings, people would come, you know, almost like a theatre, you would say. We would ask our mother, "Why did they treat these the black peoples so bad?" And she said . . . well, she didn't understand. She said that "the Lord would take care of this in the future." But, she tried, she *tried*, to shield us from having hatred. That's one thing that she did, despite what was going on.

◆ ◆ ◆

**Teaster:** I was in the Armed Services four years. I was on a ship in Long Beach, California, I went overseas three times. I didn't want to come back to Mississippi after getting out of the service. I did not. I felt like I could do better, you know, if I had not come back. But my father was old, he was about seventy and my mother wasn't in the best of health. And I felt that my father really needed someone to be near and that's why I came home.

My father believed that you get by with hard work. He felt like if a person was without, it was because he had not worked hard. That was kind of the general idea I got, that you need to work harder. He had kind of gained, I'm gonna say, a false status in the community. I remember him telling my mother that some of the white people told him that he was an outstanding citizen. But they never encouraged him to vote. My father didn't really want me to get too involved in the civil rights. He felt that it will cause so much trouble, that it would be best for me to try to go along with the status quo.

During this time, I had a brother was living in Memphis. He was the vice president of one of the branches in the NAACP in Memphis. And at this time Mr. Henry Reaves and them was having a voter's registration drive going on in Macedonia CME Church, and they invited my brother to come over and talk. And so my brother came out. My father found out about it and he came over here, this very house. And he said that he didn't want me going over there, just didn't want me going over there. "You're subject to get shot," that's what he said. He just felt like to try to avoid having conflict, you might say.

**Frances:** He was afraid for our lives. And that was one thing that kind of kept me shied away, you know. I'll tell you how it got started that we got involved. Somebody was hiring to survey land. This guy, I don't remember his name, came by and talked to my husband. He brought a big notebook, saying, "Hey, you a good guy, we want you to do this. We will hire you." And from that point, my husband said, "Let's go to the meetings." He knew that they was trying to set him up as what we call a "good nigger." And so from that point on, that's how we really got involved in civil rights. We started going to all the meetings. But I kind of done the work behind the scenes, as much as I can. The reason we had as many meetings held at Samuel's Chapel Church is because I pushed for them.

**Interviewer:** *There were some real conflicts among the deacons at Samuel's Chapel over allowing the church to be used.*

**Teaster:** I will say the older deacons, they did not want to. You know, it was three of us and I could kind of overpower the other three. And so I had a majority, I wasn't afraid to buck up, because the majority of the congregation was with me, and I knew that they were.

◆ ◆ ◆

**Teaster:** Shortly after my father, you know, passed, I had two people call and tell me you're going to have a hard time staying here among these white peoples. Said, "You're going to have to be careful," I was told that. People would come up to my driveway, turn around, and back up, you know. Make noises. I would never get up to go check on it, but I believe they were doing this to harass me or

Teaster and Frances Baird. Courtesy of the Baird family.

to get me to come out or something. That's the way that I took it. I never slept with a gun by my bed or anything. Wasn't afraid that someone would break in or do something. I just never was afraid. By me not being a large farm, I did not have to make any huge loans. I was fairly well independent you might say. That was one thing that kind of kept me out of the grip of them.[12]

I had an experience I hadn't told my wife about it. I hope she won't leave me now when I tell her. [Laughs.] This was in '74. I had been harassed a lot of times and didn't tell her. In '74, now she going to remember this, but the full extent of it, I never shared with her. On the Fourth of July of '74, we came home that night. We'd been out for a picnic. It was such a foul odor when we got in that night, we couldn't hardly stay in the house. And we couldn't figure out what was causing it, and we got up and looked the next morning. It was a great, big black hound dog, dead, right by our window. And I heard the implication that if you see a black dog around your door, that means that mean a black dead *man*. I never told my wife.

**Interviewer:** *Why did you decide to get involved?*

**Teaster:** Well, I just could not . . . I felt like I'd be going against my people, you know? Because a lot of time Mr. Henry Reaves would drive around through the county, and he was trying to get people to vote. And I knew that they were trying to do something to help the mass of people. I felt like, "Now, I could get a job that would benefit me, you know?" But I felt like I'd be going against the cause that they were trying to promote. To make things better for black people. And I just could not go against their wish.

◆   ◆   ◆

**Teaster:** I failed my voter registration test several times. They said I didn't pass it. I remember going at *least* two or three times. And then they would print my name in the *Southern Advocate*.[13] Voting is why I'm glad that I had the attitude as early as I did. I could have gotten in on the easy side if I had stayed with the other side, so to speak. As I look back, I know that this was a result of people who gave their life for this. People who marched, who sweated, who lost blood. Many made that sacrifice for this.

**Frances:** We have become complacent in that we can hardly get our young people out to vote. Or register. And once they register, getting them out to vote. And we have a long way to go in that area, because after I registered, I felt power. It's power in voting. And if we can get our young people to understand that, it would be a big help.

**Interviewer:** *Mr. Baird, if your father were to come back and say to you, "I told you not to get involved in this," what would you say?*

**Teaster:** I would just tell him . . . I was looking forward to a change. And I *wanted* a change. I wanted to be a part of this change, and I could not turn my back on the people who really could look further ahead. I had a feeling all along that he knew that things weren't right, but rather than to try to straighten it out and risk anything, he figured that he would rather just put up with what was going on. And I would try to explain to him that I wanted a better way of life.

# Loyal and Thelma Thompson

## 1923–2000 (Loyal); 1932–2019 (Thelma)

---

Interviewed December 1995, Lamar, Mississippi, by Aviva Futorian, Roy DeBerry, and Wilbur Colom

---

*Both grandchildren of enslaved persons, Mr. and Mrs. Thompson were lead-ers of the local civil rights movement in Benton County. In addition to helping found the Benton County Citizens Club, they owned eighty acres of land in 1964 and were among the first parents to send their children to desegregate the white school. Mrs. Thompson was among a group of women to integrate a local café, and Mr. Thompson, a bus driver for the county school district, was instrumental in delivering the* Benton County Freedom Train *to other active members of the movement. He was chairman of the biracial committee for the Citizens Club. Someone put a dead fox at his office door in the courthouse, an act that did not discourage him. He was described by several people as one of the bravest men they knew. At the height of the movement in 1964, he was photographed holding a rifle in* Look *magazine, an experience that haunted him the rest of his life.*

◆ ◆ ◆

**Loyal:** I can't remember the date, but I believe it was at Mount Zion Church. The first contact with civil rights volunteers from the North was made. We were interested in getting more rights as a people and that's the reason—we had heard about it, and we was going to see. We was like the man that heard about Jesus, he was going to see what was going on. When they first came in here they had more concern about getting blacks to vote. That was their first step they made—getting them registered. Now I think that was what we heard most of that night about who was gonna haul 'em and who would go and all that kind of thing.

It musta been '64. I remember Mr. Weber and Mr. Cole, we went in to register the same time. We had to fill out applications, and if you didn't pass this application you couldn't register. So I was the only one passed that day, the two teachers failed. If anybody was gonna fail, look like it should been I; I wasn't a teacher. But it felt good because it was a privilege I hadn't ever had.

**Interviewer:** *Why did you want Loyal Jr. to integrate Ashland school?*

**Thelma:** I felt that we had to stand up for our rights and it looked like the white children were being taught better. I figured that maybe he would be taught better too, you know.

**Loyal:** If I'm at the same table with you, and you eat steak, I'll eat some too. So that's why I carried him on up there. My job [for the Citizens Club] was hauling the students up there. The day the students registered, I hauled students all that day. Everybody in Ashland was out there. They had lined up across the front of the school, a line of white men and women, boys and girls. So when I got out to go in with him, we had to push 'em apart to get through to go into the office.

**Thelma:** Loyal Jr. was looking forward to it. He made a lot of preparation getting ready to go there. Get his books together, his clothes fixed. He wanted us to buy him a briefcase to tote all his stuff in. He was just looking forward to doing it. They harassed him pretty good, but he was determined to stay in there. One thing we would tell him-not to pick on nobody. Don't pick, don't meddle, but if somebody keep messing at you and won't stop, if you have to fight 'em, I said, "Give 'em a good one." On one occasion he was comin' to the house, and a girl on the bus had picked up a big walnut. And the bus passed and this girl threw that walnut and hit him with it. He said it hurt, but he stayed on in school. And he *kept* that walnut. And whenever he'd come home for a reunion, he'd have that walnut.

Only time it kind of worried me was when he went to Jackson with a group—spring or summer of '65[14]—and they arrested him and hauled them off and put 'em in this cow barn. They was down there for about ten days in there. It made him more determined. He came home and he looked pretty gaunt, it was hot and everything. He didn't back down.

**Interviewer:** *What role did you play in the* Freedom Train?

**Loyal:** Delivering them mostly. We had people to do all printing and all that kind of stuff. I would deliver 'em. I would deliver some and I would have some

Loyal and Thelma Thompson. Courtesy of Frank Cieciorka.

Loyal Thompson at a Citizens Club meeting. Courtesy of Frank Cieciorka.

Loyal Thompson from *Look* magazine. Courtesy of Aviva Futorian.

Loyal Thompson Jr. Courtesy of the Thompson family.

members of my section deliver some, we got 'em out. I was elected captain of one of the sections, and I was the chairman of the Citizens Club. Meeting with those different committees of the county and supervisors and educational board—that's some of the greatest memories. We go in to meet with four or five, and it'd turn into fifteen and twenty. People just coming to see what was going on.

**Thelma:** We was at a meeting and we decided that night who would go the Kudzu Café. I was one who said we would go, and Beulah Mae Ayers said she would go, Delilah Evans, the Judge girl, and Mizz Jones said we ought to go. So we went in the café up there early one morning, the café over on the north side of Ashland. We was planning out what we would do if they attacked us or something, you know. We went in, there wasn't anyone in there but this one man. He says, "The cooks hadn't come in." Didn't have anyone to serve us, so we offered to cook. [Laughter.] I think the workers was in the back, but they didn't show at first. Finally some come and cooked, they cooked us some greasy eggs and bacon, toast and coffee and we ate.

And then a young white lady, she come in wantin' us to go down to a place on down further from that café, Chick Autry's place. See, mostly men was in there. I guess she figured if, see, it was all women, we went in there maybe . . . ain't no telling what would happen to us, you know. So when we come out of the café, Mr. Henry Reaves come out from behind a building wanting to know, "What happened? What *happened*?" you know. [Laughter.] We told we were served and everything, but he advised us not to go in Chick's Place. So we didn't go in there. We come on out, but before we get to the café, we stopped at the ABC Shirt Factory and put in an application, 'cause weren't any blacks working in that factory, it was all-white. And any black was hired in there they would treat 'em so rough they would quit.

**Interviewer:** *Did any of you get hired?*

**Thelma:** Nah, the factory done went out, it closed.

**Loyal:** I remember there's supposed to have been a meeting one night in Ashland. None of my members come out to be with me. I believe we had seven whites and seven blacks meet to sort of sit down and iron out things. So I went to this meeting, to the place where we supposed to meet, where the old Ashland bank used to be. When I walked in the lights was so dim you couldn't recognize a person ten yards from you. And one man met me there, that was Hamer McKenzie. So we stayed there a few minutes and then left after nobody else come. The next morning, I went back to Ashland, and by my door, there was a dead fox laying in the door, signifying what could happen, you know.

**Thelma:** It was so much harassing going on. The Klan would begin to travel and they was shooting in peoples' yards and sheets over their head—

**Loyal:** I went to a dentist in Holly Springs and when I walked in he asked me, "What are you doing down here?" I said, "I want to get my teeth pulled," and he told me, he said, "You get off the streets. There's guns pointed at you from every direction. They'll take you out," he said. I said, "Well, look, one thing 'bout that. They didn't give me my life and until God get ready, they can't take it." So I just kept on going. Ain't but one time I was a little bit afraid is when we came from a meeting over near the Louisiana Line. We went through Indianola and picked up some of the workers there and went on round to this meeting of the Mississippi Freedom Democratic Party.[15] We's comin' back through Senatobia and Tunica, and we had to dodge the highway patrol and get out of there. They's waiting on us. I think one got caught that night put in jail, but they got him out the next day.

◆ ◆ ◆

**Loyal:** Some people here from *Look* magazine, they took pictures of us picking peas out here, and I was sitting on my own porch with my shotgun cross my belt and they took that picture, and it was saying something down below my name—

**Thelma:** It said, "Mr. Thompson hasn't shot his 12-gauge shotgun in the air. At least not *yet*."[16]

**Loyal:** People called me from California and other places about that picture. That picture give me a hard way to go. I couldn't find work! Couldn't find work. I went to Collierville the month after. When they discovered who I was—boom. I went to Olive Branch for factory work, about a month—boom. That picture messed me up. I would go to a place to be hired and the man look out the office and see me and say naw . . .

**Interviewer:** *When all was said and done, was it worth it?*

**Loyal:** Yes, it was. It was worth it. Sometimes I said, "Lord why me?" But it's got to be somebody.

# Henry Leake

## 1921–2019

Interviewed September 2012, Chicago, Illinois, by Aviva Futorian and John Lyons

*When his parents died young, Mr. Leake's uncle, Henry Reaves, adopted him. Raised in Benton County and a veteran of World War II, he was part of the Great Migration north and settled in Chicago, where he owned a barbershop for decades. His work ethic and entrepreneurial spirit were no doubt influenced by Mr. Reaves. "I have a PhD in living. And it didn't come from college either," he said soon after sitting down with us in his living room on the south side of Chicago.*

◆ ◆ ◆

My dad and mother died with tuberculosis. My dad was forty-two years old, my mother was twenty-nine. Henry Reaves was my mother's brother. And he kind of inherited us, because he wasn't married. So they asked him to take us, and he did.

He was a very generous man, and he looked out for us pretty well. Life was pretty good. At that time, we weren't old enough to work and we was like any other child growing up in a home. Because he was a young man, not married, you know, a lot of times he wouldn't be there. We could get away with things that we couldn't get away with if he was there. It was about 1932, that's when I first started plowing, and going to the field, and doing something every day. We went to school down at Mount Zion until I was about fourteen.

He wouldn't let us work for white folks. He never said why. He just always showed us that you work for yourself. He always tried to have something for us to do. Sometimes on Saturday during the summer months, he'd tell us we could go to town. Well, instead of us going to town, we'd go to the white folks land up there, and try to make a quarter or two, to have some money.

He was a very, very good person. But he was mean. He was mean about *real* things. He would never let the white folks direct him what to do. He was always doing something . . . to pull the cover off a lot of things. He just wasn't educated. White people would've killed him if he'd been really educated.

◆ ◆ ◆

Going to different schools, that was automatic. That's something you never have to wonder about, because you know what the law was. You know your boundaries and you didn't ask about it. You never thought about it.

I remember when these guys[17] was hung, it was just a thing in the community. They was talking about it, leading up to the lynching. And they were talking, people would be talking about it, but they wouldn't talk to the kids about it. But you could hear them talking to each other. You knew, if you was old enough. You knew that it was the wrong thing for them to do. But what could you do about it? That's the main thing, there was nothing to do about it.

◆ ◆ ◆

When I left Benton County, I was seventeen. Being the son of a veteran, the government paid to go to MIC.[18] We had college kids, high school kids all on the same campus. And, it was a boarding school, had dormitories. I lived in the dormitory. I was there from when I was seventeen and I must've been twenty when I left. I got married to Jane when I was eighteen. She was in the dorm at Rust College. After we got married, the war broke out in 1941. And that means people got scattered and going different places. So we separated, and they called me into the service. I was drafted and went to Camp Shelby, near Hattiesburg, Mississippi. And, from there, I went to Fort Eustis, Virginia, for my basic training. After that, I went to Fort Stewart, Georgia, for advanced training. And after that, before I went overseas, I went to Fort Leonard Wood, Missouri. And from there, to Liverpool England.

I was in the service for forty-eight months. That was a joyous time because I wanted to see the world. Until you get up there and get in it. I was all over, saw a lot of action. When you get in it, your mind runs back home, that you might not get back there.

We never thought about fighting for freedom. Maybe some of the older soldiers did. But when you're eighteen, nineteen, twenty years old, you don't think about what you're fighting for.

Henry Leake in the service. Courtesy of the Reaves
family.

**Interviewer:** *During your time in Europe, did you notice any difference between
how you were treated by white Europeans versus how you were treated by white
Americans?*

That's very noticeable because—you start looking for women, you understand?
And all of them was white. You know, you couldn't do that back home. So, you
noticed a difference. Because, you looking for a girlfriend on Sunday when
you ain't doing nothing. You know it's going to be a white girl, if it be one.
And nobody never said, "No, you couldn't." The people in England never said
anything about it. People in France, they didn't say anything about it.

◆ ◆ ◆

I come to Chicago in '46. I went to school under the GI Bill, and then got my
license. And I opened my own business. I went to barber school; it took me
about two years to get my license.

   In 1946, when I came here, you could tell there was a difference. I almost seen
more racism in Chicago than I have ever seen in Mississippi. White people here
in Chicago, as far as I'm concerned, you think that they are your friend. You

think that they are all right with you. But they'll let you down when it comes
to white versus black. They'll just go against you, in any situation.

You got to have somebody to keep pressing, like Uncle Henry had done.
I'm saying he kept pressing and pressing. I never started really thinking about
the conditions of this country until television got to be plentiful. Then you
started looking at things and what was going on and all that. 1964, that's when
I really got interested in what was going on. Stokely Carmichael, he come to
one of our meetings once, and I got a chance to meet him. And, you know,
listen to his speech, to the things he was saying. That kind of woke me up to
what was really going on.

**Interviewer:** *When you go back to Mississippi these days, do you see a difference?*

Oh, yes. It's a wonderful experience. I enjoy going back there. because, you see
blacks in so many different spots that they weren't allowed to walk in. They're
sheriffs, and heads of different organizations—I never thought that would ever
happen. I never thought I'd . . . if I lived to get 150, I never thought I would live
to see a black president. Oh, that was such a surprise to me.

# Walter Reaves

## Born 1923

Interviewed December 1995, Ashland, Mississippi, by Aviva Futorian and Wilbur Colom

*Independent and fiercely outspoken, Mr. Reaves has activism built into his DNA. He is the nephew of both Charlie and Henry Reaves, two of the leaders of the movement, and sent his children to desegregate the Ashland School. A retired plumber and electrician, he was himself one of the leaders of the movement in Benton County. He welcomed us into his home for this conversation.*

◆ ◆ ◆

My daddy told us that it wasn't no difference in black people and white people. He pointed out a few black folks that was working for white people and needed to have been working for themselves. What my daddy called it was "flunking for white folks." That some blacks had went to the white person's house and worked in their garden, worked in their flower bed, and were just a real general flunky for the white people. And he told us that he didn't want us to ever do that. He said, "You can get out there and work for yourself. You can have something just like they can." And I reckon that's the reason I'm sittin' in my own house.

◆ ◆ ◆

Our folks, black folks, had no high schools, they only covered eight grades. The citizens here in the county built the first high school that black folks had. No government money. In the latter part of '43, I believe. My daddy had a truck and we drove to Grenada, Mississippi, and we hauled enough lumber to just about build the school. My father, me, and my brother hauled gravel. We would take a pick and a shovel, pick it up, and load it on the truck. Me and my brother

30

made two loads a day and that's what they poured the footing for Old Salem School. Everybody joined in and helped transport that lumber, went down and worked. It was no trouble to get somebody to join in, 'cause we didn't have a high school. I don't know how we done it, but we ran our own buses. We ran those buses from '46 up until they opened Old Salem School where it is now.

**Interviewer:** *John Farese* [the county attorney] *said that the county did it because they didn't want black children going to white schools and they figured if they built their own school, they wouldn't have to go to the white school.*

Farese was the type person that tried to avoid integrating. He pretty well controlled everything. Before I even knowed that integration was in existence, he done things for me because he knew it was coming up. But when integration started, he pointed those things out to me—what he had did for me. And he didn't just out and say, "I don't want you to integrate," but he talked in that direction. In fact, he called me to his office one day. It had to be '64 or '65, before school integration. When I went in, he was on one side of the table. He reached over and shook my hand and he said, "Listen, I have stuck my neck out, and you can help me. If you don't help me, I'm gonna get it chopped off." And right through those words, I could see where he was driving. He wanted me to say, "I don't want to integrate." And I said to him, "Mr. Farese, if I do what you want me to do, I'll going against myself plus I'll be going against my people, and I don't know nothing else to tell you, but you have to get it chopped off." I was looking right at him just like I'm looking at you. And when I said that to him, he said, "Well!" He grinned. He got red, and then he got white. It just look like it done him back, so he didn't have nothing else to say. So I got up and left. Told him, "I'll see you later." I give him them words and that was the last time that he called me to his office.

◆ ◆ ◆

Henry Reaves was my uncle. Way back before anything got started, he attended meetings, in Jackson, Mississippi Delta, and other places. He was a member of the NAACP before I ever knowed the organization was going on. When it come time for me to register to vote, he told me to pay my poll tax for two years, get two poll tax receipts, and I can go up and register. So I went up and registered.

I attended every meeting that I could make. Wherever it was. Jackson, I even attended civil rights meetings in Greenwood, Mississippi. The only time I ever been to Greenwood. I went to a lot of places in Mississippi that I had never been during those times. When I started attending those meetings, shoot, it's just like going to church with me. Anywhere one was, I would go.

There was a meeting at Samuel's Chapel Church, I can't describe the date nor the time. It was concerning integrating of the school. Mr. Jack Elmore, who was a concerned citizen, but he always lean toward the white people. He made a talk at this meeting saying that black people was going too fast. He talked for probably twenty or thirty minutes. When he sat down, Aviva Futorian, she taken the floor and she started off with, "I don't see how anyone could say that you're going too fast when you already a hundred years behind."

Now at the beginning of the integration, they had grades one, two, three, and twelve. So they had this Freedom of Choice, that if a child had a sister or brother they could transfer over to the same school. So Imogene, my oldest daughter, integrated the seventh grade, Murray and Mary Jane integrated the fifth grades. On the morning that I taken them over to Ashland, I called the school personnel and told them I was coming with them. When I arrived at the school, there was two fifth grade teachers there. And when I got there they had decided between the two teachers who was gon' take the boy and who was gon' take the girl 'cause they both was in the fifth grade. But Imogene, she's the only one seventh grade teacher there so she had no problem then. So she integrated.

**Interviewer:** *Was there any question that they should attend?*

I didn't have that in mind. They would get a better education over at Ashland School. To sit in right with the white children.

I instructed my kids, the three that went over to Ashland, "Look, you are going over to get an education. You're not going there to raise a disturbance with nobody. You go over and you do what you suppose to do. If they call you 'nigger,' that's all right. Make no difference what they call you. That ain't gon' hurt you. If they spit on you, that's all right. It ain't gon' hurt you . . . but now if he hit you, you better hit him back." I give 'em them instructions when they left home before I taken them over. So I had no problems.

Imogene talked about it sometimes, you know, going to meeting and things. She was right with me wherever I went. When she could go, you know, I would let her go.

I lost jobs, yeah. They just didn't call me to do any work for them. Before integration, I found that I had a white guy that didn't want me to work at his house. I worked for a white man that was doing wiring and plumbing, James Norton McGill. Now McGill was nice enough to tell me things. So he told me this white guy wanted him to do some plumbing for him, but he told him, "Now the day you gonna work in my house, let your helper go fishing." McGill said to me, "I told him, 'He works for me and if you don't want him, then you

Imogene Reaves, daughter of Walter.
Courtesy of Aviva Futorian.

Walter Reaves. Courtesy of Frank
Cieciorka.

don't want me.'" So, you know, I wouldn't even thought the guy would have said those words.

◆ ◆ ◆

I don't remember what year it was, but I was with the group that went into Autry's Café. The group met and formed. Some went inside. I stayed outside to make sure I know what went on outside.

**Interviewer:** *You were the getaway car?*

Yes, I was outside watching to see what was gonna go on. So far as anything happening, people was just looking. People come out to their stores and was looking towards the café but so far as anything happening, nothing happened. I believe they was served.

We had this little office over at Carey Tipler's place. Somebody would write it up and we'd run the printing machine and print the *Freedom Train* up. Tell you the truth, I don't know how the machine went. I know we ran it. Maybe three of four of us. Some worked the machine and then some of 'em stapled 'em together. Four or five people worked maybe half a day. We mostly printed them on a Saturday, I believe, and I'd take so many and distribute them out to different people. Whoever was interested in it. I'd offer it 'em whether they wanted it or not. The most of them always took the *Freedom Train*.

The first open civil rights meeting that was held at Ripley, she[19] [Fannie Lou Hamer] was key speaker. She said that she was sick and tired of the southern way of life—that it just made her sick and tired. That night after we left there, that's when the church burned down. She really talked good that night.

The first service after they started the church back, it was Christmas Day. I was right there. We had eight-inch blocks sitting up and had boards on them blocks. We was on a front bench, we was on the front row.

**Interviewer:** *Was there ever a time that you had any questions about whether it was worth it?*

No, no. I was right. I was right in what I was doing working in civil rights so, I wasn't gonna go back.

# Ginevera Reaves

## 1923–2002

Interviewed December 1995, outside of Ashland, Mississippi, by Aviva Futorian and Roy DeBerry

*The mother of two children and wife of Henry Reaves, Mrs. Reaves worked in various capacities in the Benton County School System, eventually gaining a BS in school administration from the University of Chicago in 1954. She was an integral part of the Benton County Citizens Club, an organization her husband founded. She was also the cousin of Aaron Henry, the state NAACP leader from Mississippi. Mr. S. T. Nero, her father, was a prominent educator and activist who taught Latin at Rosenwald High School in Holly Springs, Mississippi. She talked with us in the living room of her house, which was a hotbed of activity during the movement.*

◆ ◆ ◆

I met a young man in Jackson, Mississippi. I said I was from Benton County. He says, "There hasn't been but one person there that's ever been *out* of Benton County." I say, "Who was that?" He said, "Henry Reaves." [Laughter.] Well, Henry always made contact. Much of what went on in Benton County and in the state of Mississippi came through Henry. Church, NAACP, anything that meant being human, Henry was gonna be a part of it. And he wanted that for everyone's children.

Henry had organized the Citizens Club in the early sixties and that was to bring the blacks together. It was Henry, Charlie Reaves, Eugene and Ellie Steward, Annie Mae Weber, Walter Weber, Sarah Washington, Jessie Crawford. The point we were concerned with was being citizens and not being represented as it relates to making decisions. And you have to be a voter in order to make decisions. And the point was to get a representative number of blacks to vote.

Ginevera Reaves. Courtesy of the
Reaves family.

Henry and Ginevera Reaves. Courtesy of
the Reaves family.

Naomi Reaves. Courtesy of the Reaves family.

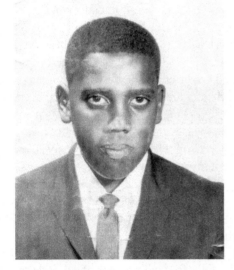

Henry Reaves Jr. (Sonny). Courtesy of the Reaves family.

**Interviewer:** *When was the first time you had any connection to the civil rights volunteers in 1964?*

It was a gang of them out here at the house, I don't know how many. I always considered my daddy, S. T. Nero, a real brave man, and he was. He lived in Holly Springs, but he came out here. He was here that Sunday when everybody was out here. He supported everything, but he had a lot of concern for me and Henry. He didn't want anything to happen. He knew people would do mean things. They knew Henry was one of the leaders, and they felt like this was the place to come. We had several blacks come in and meet the SNCC volunteers. It was just sort of like a fellowship to me. They wanted to know what they were doing in there, and a lot of them were afraid. Then, gradually, they began to shake this off. You know, the *fear*. And they begin to sort of come out and be concerned about themselves, come to meetings, and learn more about what was going on.

We would meet at different churches, sometime at Mount Zion and sometimes at Greenwood. Local people were fascinated. It was something new and they just sort of pitched right in. They just loved Pete Cummings. Pete could lead them off almost any place. He was young, he was vibrant, he was friendly, he cared. And they sensed that, you know. People sense when you are genial, real. I always say they have built-in antennas, they sense when you're sincere and faking something. I felt that he was very sincere in what he was doing.

◆ ◆ ◆

I served as coach for the basketball teams (girls and boys), guidance counselor, served as assistant principal, principal. In other words I worked in the public schools here for about fifteen years. And I had been attending civil rights meetings in Jackson, Mississippi; Mound Bayou, Holly Springs. It was hinted at from the whites to other blacks that I should not be attending those meetings and that I would perhaps lose my job. And, of course, I let them know that they didn't make my decisions. In other words, as long as I was working, they paid me. I bought my transportation, bought my gas, and my husband and I made decisions. Nobody else made our decisions. So, we felt at liberty to go any place that we wanted to as long as we were not infringing upon the rights of others. In March, you would know whether you were coming back or not. So I had not been notified that I was coming back. They just simply didn't rehire me.

I believe somebody called me and told me that Aviva has been arrested.[20] I got right out and I had told them that I wanted to see her. They let me in, I talked to her, and wasn't but a minute that I was in there. Different folks come pulling up with boots on and coveralls, folks from all across the field, and the road was full of people.

Now this is really when they became concerned about the schools. They were not too particular about whites dictating to their children and they felt like Mr. Foster[21] should have been man enough to say yes or no on his own. The Citizens Club went in to talk to Mr. Foster. He was hedging.

I said, "Mr. Foster, you disappoint me." He was just flimsy, you know? No backbone at all. We wanted a school that the white man wasn't sitting over our children *and* the principal too. It was parents meeting, discussing their concerns. And all the parents made some demands asking that Foster stand up and be a principal on his own. And if he didn't, they would have to take their children out of school.

**Interviewer:** *And the Citizens Club voted to boycott the school?*

Right. The boycott lasted three or four weeks. So Freedom Schools[22] started. Freedom School was sure to get some information concerning self-concept, black history, and also the basics as it related to their regular curriculum. Because when this was over, no one wanted to be behind. A lot of it dealt with self-concept. Making you cognizant of what's around and about you and those things that are important in life. Those children were really concerned about what's happening. They learned how to look at things to analyze, make connections, and think about what's going on. I was sort of proud of those students like Alberta Tipler, Ernestine Scott, and those Reaves children. They knew what their parents were doing and what the civil rights workers were trying to do. Make things better.

# William Bullock

## Born 1931

Interviewed September 2013, Ashland, Mississippi, by Aviva Futorian, Roy DeBerry, and John Lyons

*The son of sharecroppers, Mr. Bullock was active in the movement. His early life was nomadic as his parents moved from farm to farm. As an adult, he and his wife briefly moved to Indianapolis, Indiana, to be with her family before returning to Benton County, eventually owning their own property. "She done the mortgage, my wife. Filled the application out and got it passed, and that's the way I come by this home." He sat down with us under an oak tree in his front yard.*

◆ ◆ ◆

Sharecropping means that when you're on a white person's place, regardless of what you make—how many bales of cotton—they would get half of it. And if they'd get half of it, then most of the time when you go to settle up, you wouldn't get a dime. You'd always be three or four hundred dollars in the hole.

I went to Shiloh School. I guess I went there from six to twelve years old. But I didn't get no real education. The white people then, if you stayed on their place and got ready to pick cotton, they didn't want us blacks to go to school. They wanted us to be out there picking that cotton. But *their* kids could go to school. Didn't care if the cotton was running over. But people that's black staying on as sharecroppers, we had to do what they said, or we had to be looking for another place to stay. And wouldn't know where it was going to be. If you couldn't miss school, your folks had to move.

I can' speak for other counties, but I can speak for Benton County. I would say around twelve years old, coming up here, when we'd go to a white person's house, you had to tip your hat or cap. They didn't really want no black person coming to the front door. If you were working for him, the white person, when twelve o'clock come for lunch, you had to sit out here, outside, wait till they get through eating. Then if they didn't offer you in the house, they'd bring you your food outside. That's true. You couldn't eat with them. My parents always told me, "You do what Mr. So-and-So tells you to do, because we ain't got nowhere to stay."

I got five boys. If I stayed on a white man's place and he says, "These your boys? What they doing?" I say, "They got a little job." He says, "Well, if they can't help me tomorrow, you got to move." I thought it was bad. But, right then, just a few black folks had their own land. And under that system, you didn't have nowhere to go. You had to go with it, or find you somewhere else to go. That's no lie. I'm telling you the facts from my heart. You had to move.

◆ ◆ ◆

Racial violence in Benton County [a long pause]. Yeah. You had to be real good. *Extra* good. And even then sometimes . . . I'm talking about Pete Harris. I'll tell you what happened. Pete Harris, he worked up here at the Ashland Clinic. There was a white lady, and he drove her around to check sick peoples, if they needed a shot or something. One Friday, right up here on the edge of town, I was plowing mules. And he comes by here, walking. He went right over here. That night, they killed him. Put him right out there in the pond for driving this white lady around. I was at church that Sunday when they come in, saying the water is smelling so bad. When they got ready to bury him, you couldn't look at his body. He stayed in that water from Friday night to late that Sunday. He was a real good, young fella. But like I said, they didn't want him to be playing that game.

I went to church with Mr. Henry Reaves some. He come by, asking us to register to vote. And we did. We had to take a test, also pay a poll tax. He got out to the blacks and asked them to vote. And that made a change in life to me. Everybody else in this county, especially blacks, seemed like they was scared to try to do anything. They scared they may lose their life, or their family, because all that was going on here in Benton County. And that's life. I ain't got no good book learning. But I try to pitch it out the best I know it. And Mr. Reaves—I think he done his part. When I went to the civil rights meetings, I went to Macedonia, I went to Samuel's Chapel.[23] He asked for us to get out and do things to help ourselves. We needed him. We needed to control ourselves. Any time you help yourself is good. But so many blacks was scared. And even then, I couldn't rest good. I didn't know if they'd burn me down.

◆ ◆ ◆

I tell my kids now how we come up. And they say, "Dad, I wouldn't have stayed there." I said, "What choice do you have? Where could you go?" You're broke, ain't got a penny. What could you do about it? Nothing. You had to take it. So it's been rough. But the Lord let me get eighty-two years old. I lived through that. And I thank the Lord for it. And He blessed us. He has been kind as we moved in and out.

# Jessie and Alverna Crawford

## 1918–2007 (Jessie); 1918–2012 (Alverna)

Interviewed November 2004, Lamar, Mississippi, by Aviva Futorian and John Lyons

*Although he was a founding member of the Benton County Citizens Club, Mr. and Mrs. Crawford were not heavily involved in the movement until the 1960s, after Freedom Summer. Several factors kept them from becoming active at first, primarily transportation (they couldn't easily go to meetings) and fear. By no means were they unique in that response. Once the movement gained momentum, they became participants. High school sweethearts, they sat down together with us on their farm, which they've owned since 1967.*

◆ ◆ ◆

**Jessie:** I didn't get no farther than fourth grade. It was a bunch of us children, there was fifteen of us in the family. I mostly stayed around, cutting wood, and tried to sell wood to feed the rest of the children. Doing little jobs, working with the white folks on the fences and things. Picking cotton, yeah. I worked for an old white man, I got forty-five cents a day for the hours from sunup to sundown. I told one of my grandgirls that the other day. I tell them, "Y'all better take care of what you make, 'cause things don't stay this way all the time."

**Alverna:** They couldn't believe that!

**Jessie:** They couldn't believe that.

**Alverna:** Our own children couldn't believe that we got forty or fifty cents a day. I stayed in school till the eighth grade. I went one year in high school and got married to him. We been married sixty years, we've always been farmers.

**Jessie:** I only have five acres now. I used to have more, when I bought this land in 1967, I borrowed the money from the FHA.[24]

**Interviewer:** *When you were growing up did you hear of any kind of racial violence in Benton County?*

**Alverna:** I know a man, they killed him. Went by Pete Harris, he lived here in Ashland. And somebody came to where he lived one night and called him out and he never come back. He was working at the health department out there, in that clinic. It was back in the '40s, 'cause they had just built the clinics in Ashland. And back in them days, clinic folks would go to church and give people these shots, you know. And he used to drive around with a white lady, I remember, he used to drive her around. He cleaned up around the clinic and then when they went out he would always ride with them. Sometimes they had him driving. That's the only reason I know they could have got him.

**Jessie:** A black man couldn't ride beside a white woman or else white men were going to do something to them. And he was just working up there with them, and maybe he just came around handling her bags, maybe he opened the car door for her when he stopped. And them white men wasn't going to stand for it. And the gang just got him. I don't think he had been shot. I don't know what they did to him, but his body had come up after a couple of days in the pond.

◆  ◆  ◆

**Jessie:** I wasn't more than twelve or fourteen years old. These two white fellows got robbed and killed and they laid it on two black boys over there in Ashland.[25] They had lynched them. That night, Papa come and told us he was going to carry us up there to see them. When we went up to see them . . . the shape we found them in . . . outside the jail, with this rope set around his neck. His tongue was hanging out of his mouth. These boys, these *young* boys. And a white guy by the name of Jim Smith—I never would forget that—come up behind me, and we were looking at them, and told my dad, "Herman, they got on pretty neckties, ain't they?" Papa just looked around at him and said, "I don't know what the hell they got on. Let's go, boys." And he took us on back. I don't really remember what he said. I think he done it to show us how they done to black people. I believe he wanted us to be careful, to be scared of them. And that's what made me be more . . . *not* afraid of white folks anymore. I really wasn't afraid of them. I was mad.

**Interviewer:** *When the movement first came here, you all weren't real active. You kind of waited a little bit.*

**Alverna:** We kind of waited until the we thought the Ku Klux Klan was out the way.

**Jessie:** I don't think we had the transportation to go to those meetings at that time. But when it first come down here, we went to *all* those meetings, didn't we honey?

**Alverna:** Most of them. We used to have them at Harris Chapel, we used to have them out there at our church, Salem. Y'all had the meetings on down there at the church, and I looked down there and said, "Lord, there . . . used to be a church *full* of folks out there." I know that much. I know we went there, Harris. Most of the churches I believe had meetings, Salem and Mount Zion. But I remember a lot of the churches wouldn't . . . they wouldn't budge. It was a long time before they would let a meeting come in their church.

**Interviewer:** *Are things better now?*

**Alverna:** Well, I think we done come a long way and I think we still got a long way. You know, 'cause things is kind of better. I know they treat you a little better since we had been integrated with each other at work.

**Jessie:** Some treat you better than others. They treat you better, it's just a little bit different now.

# Chapter 2

# GENERATIONS

*One of the predominant themes of Benton Countians' involvement in the movement was to create a more equitable world for their children and the next generation. The following interviews are with some of the first, most active members of Benton County's civil rights movement, followed by interviews with their children, nephews, and nieces. The issue of school desegregation flows through these stories, as it was one of the primary battles of that time. The United States Supreme Court ordered states to end segregated education in 1954, "with all deliberate speed." More than a decade later, Mississippi was forced by the federal government to introduce "Freedom of Choice," which permitted certain black students to attend the white school. Benton County staggered this choice for various grades over a few years. The fall of 1965 saw the first black students enter Ashland, the all-white school.*

# Spence Richard

## 1929–2016

Interviewed September 2003 and October 2005, Lamar, Mississippi, by Aviva Futorian, Roy DeBerry, John Lyons, and Stephen Klein

*Were he born in a different time and place, Mr. Richard could have been a professor of philosophy. Unlike many in his generation, he viewed education as crucial. A widower for over almost twenty years, he and his wife raised nine children, eight of whom finished college. He sharecropped, then later farmed his own land and also worked for the Marshall County School System as a maintenance man. He became active in the movement in the mid-1960s and sent his children to desegregate Ashland School. His activity in the movement as a sharecropper was especially risky as the family could have been kicked off the land at any point. We talked with him twice at his home, with some of his family members occasionally sitting in.*

◆ ◆ ◆

My mother had seven children, one girl and six boys. The girl died when she was a baby and the other brother died when he was about a year old. Five of us lived to get grown. Two of those already passed away, and I'm seventy-six. So I guess I got one foot in the grave and another one on a banana peel.

My daddy don't remember his daddy. And his mamma died early. So he went to work for the Hamers[1] at an early age. White people almost raised him. He didn't own any land; he was a sharecropper with the Hamers. How did that work? The man fronted the mule. He fed us. Bought us clothes. And he got half of the crop we made. If we made ten bales of cotton, he got five. We got five and then he'd take out any expenses out of our half and then if we had anything left then he would give us that. He got his part, you might say, clear.

48

But we paid for our part outta what we made. Sometimes we cleared somethin', and sometimes we didn't.

As my brothers got old enough, Daddy hired them out to the white man. They had a little house they slept in. And they fed them but they didn't get to come home until Saturday. In other words, I never really lived in the house with my brothers, only on the weekends. I was the only one that he didn't hire out. Daddy was afraid to tell the white man, "No, I ain't gonna hire my son out this year." And I remember one time my brother Steve come and told my daddy a white man cussed at him or somethin' in the field. My daddy's response to that was: "We gotta do what these white folks say to do."

My daddy taught me something, but he don't know he did. When a white man came to our house or in the field where he was, Daddy wouldn't look at him in the face. He would get his stick and work on the ground while the white man was talking. And everything the white man said to him, "Yes, sir." He wouldn't look at him. Just, "Yes, sir." I said, "Why you don't look at the white man?" I thought, "When I get to be a man, I'm gonna *look* at him when I talk to him." But my daddy, see, my daddy come up different than me. He came up under those Reconstruction Days.[2]

**Interviewer:** *What incidents have you heard of involving racial violence in Benton County?*

Houey and that other man,[3] they were hanged across the four-lane highway. Daddy went to Michigan City in a wagon after it happened. Ain't nobody around but me and him in the wagon. I guess folks was in the field. And he said, "See them trees up there? That's where they hanged those men." He says, "Now you can look up in them trees when you get there, but I'm not." So when he got up to them trees, I looked up and there was a piece of rope hanging there. Daddy wouldn't even look. When he got to that tree he just . . . he looked straight down at the road.

So he stood in fear of the white man. Not only him, but most blacks back then stood in fear of him. Because if he talked up for himself, he's subject to punishment, they'd do something to him. It's kind of tough to talk about, but he come up in a rough time.

◆   ◆   ◆

The people Daddy was working for, it didn't make any difference if he had an education or not. And I guess he thought that was all right for him not to want one. So when he married and had us, he felt the same way towards us as

Spence Richard. Courtesy of the Richard family.

Spence Richard, after his conversation with coeditors Stephen Klein and Aviva Futorian. Courtesy of John Lyons.

far as I'm concerned. My daddy didn't believe in education. Now my momma, she did. What Momma done, I didn't realize this until she had passed away. Daddy could be out front talkin' to somebody, and I'm getting ready to go to school. And I would wanna go out the front door, she'd say, "Come here, go out this door." After she passed away, I just realized why she sent me out that back door. If Daddy saw me, he probably would have stopped me. He wouldn't let me go. And I'll tell somethin' else my momma done. Wasn't much paper back then, didn't have the money to buy it. Every once in a while, we would get what they call nowadays junk mail. She would tear that open and write my name—I hadn't been to school yet—write my name and leave a space and write it again and leave a space. I could write my name almost as good as I am now before I even went to school the first day. My momma believed in education.

I thought at one time I couldn't remember things. I thought if I read a paragraph, it'd just go away. My shop teacher, that man started me to believe I could think. That teacher got my attention when he done this. Not only mine, but about twenty boys. The teacher had a brother somewhere, his son got in trouble. And his brother wrote him a letter and was telling him about his son in trouble. He said, "Fellas, I'll let all of you all read this letter. It's none of your business, but I'm going to pass it around to every one of you." That *wasn't* our business, what was in that letter, but he was just seeing, how could we think? This boy read it, that boy read it. It moved around quickly. Then he said, "Give it back to me." He put it back in his pocket, went on with the class. The next morning when he got to class, he wanted to know, "Who all remembered what was on that letter?" Every boy in the room raised his hand. That started me to think I could think for myself. Then it got around to graduation time, at the end of the school year. He said, "Fellas, if you prepare yourself, jobs will hunt *you*. Otherwise, you'll hunt jobs." At that time, didn't make no sense. A job hunting me? I didn't tell the teacher that. But anyway, when my children got to be seven, eight, and ten years old, I'm talking about I'd been out of school for years. It came back to me. He opened my mind.

**Interviewer:** *Most of your siblings moved out of Benton County. Why did you stay?*

I missed the army. That's what caused some of my brothers to go away. There was five of us and I never did go. I was that age for the Korean War. But they wasn't takin' anybody with children and Marsha was born during the Korean War. I got married and I moved over here on Norman McKenzie's[4] place and worked there sixteen years as a sharecropper. One day Mr. McKenzie said, "Spence, one of these days your children and our children gonna be goin' to the same school." And I said, "Mr. McKenzie, I won't live long enough to see it."

**Interviewer:** *Why did you decide to get active in the civil rights movement? Why did you go to those meetings?*

Listening to Martin Luther King Jr. on the radio. It just rang the bell for me. That man was right, and segregation was wrong. I just thought, regardless of race or color, if a person says the right thing, and do the right thing, I don't see how he can't be *treated* right. I just couldn't figure that out. I'll tell you why I went. I went mostly to learn what we were supposed to be. Humans. And I went to learn that freedom is supposed to be for all mankind. It was an education for me to go.

**Interviewer:** *Why did you want to send your kids to integrate the school?*

This Little Rock[5] deal, I admired those children that went to that school. And I said if I ever have some and they wanna integrate, I'm gonna let 'em go. If they're gonna get a better education . . . try to get the best one. I always felt that we were a little shorthanded on some stuff in these schools. I didn't tell them not to fight. I didn't tell them *to* fight. I told them this: Stay out of rough conversation with other boys and girls. So I wanted them to have a education. It was our responsibility. So I bought no new car, no new truck. I drove old stuff so I could have enough money to get 'em to school. That's an investment right there in my children. We put eight through college and the ninth one went three years and didn't finish. That's Charles [who has cerebral palsy]. Now I wish I could tell you . . . *how* I done that. You're talkin' about *thirty* some years in college with children, and I just can't, I can't come up with words to . . . we done it with very little help. We just kept our little money together.

◆  ◆  ◆

Marsha's grandma was paying Marsha's lunch bill for us, twenty-five cents a day. They didn't want Marsha to go to the high school at Ashland. When we let her go, they stopped paying her lunch bill. And Marsha wanted to go, too. I said, "You're not afraid to go, Marsha?" She said, "No sir, I'm not afraid." I said, "I'm behind you 100 percent." This shows you how afraid the black people were back then. They thought something was going to happen.

Somebody, now I don't know who, set a cross on fire, between here and that intersection down there. I happened to go down the road the next morning, there was a little cross about three foot. They had set it on fire and it had burnt down. That cross was a symbol: "We're going to get you."

**Interviewer:** *Didn't that frighten you a little?*

No! No! If I die for the right thing, let it happen. My wife always used my nickname. She said, "Harry, you don't believe in handguns, why don't you just buy you one?" I said, "Oh, well, let me think about it." I did. I thought about it for three or four days. I come to this conclusion. If I had six guns, on my truck seat, had them all cocked, if they wanted to kill me, that wouldn't stop them. That wouldn't stop them. And I believed it wouldn't. Here I am, I'm seventy-six years old now, I wouldn't give you fifty cents for the best one they make now. There's a better way. If they want to shoot me, go ahead and shoot. I believe in nonviolence. Let me ask all of you a loaded question. Is there such thing as a bad person? I don't believe there is, anymore. I've been hum-hawing over it, and I think there's some foolish people, but a *bad* person? A coward will kill you, so who's bad? But y'all didn't ask me that.

# Marsha Richard Gillespie

## Born 1951

Interviewed September 2003, Lamar, Mississippi, by Aviva Futorian and John Lyons

*The first of Spence Richard's children, Marsha Gillespie attended the Ashland School in the tenth grade, the second year of school desegregation. She later attended Jackson State University and became an English teacher, eventually working as the librarian at Ashland. She also is a manager at Walmart in Holly Springs. It quickly became clear in talking with her that Ms. Gillespie used humor to lessen the blow of the petty indignities visited upon her daily in a segregated society. She talked with us in the backyard of her father's home.*

◆ ◆ ◆

I guess the first memory of racial divide as a child was when I became aware of my dad going to civil rights meetings. We were at an all-black school and we didn't have a chance to, you know, mingle with the whites except for Mr. Norman McKenzie and his children. He owned land here in Benton County and my parents were sharecroppers who worked for Mr. McKenzie. And I remember growing up on the farm working the crops and things with my parents for Mr. McKenzie. It was not a matter of growing up and realizing that we are separate from the white children. I didn't give them a thought, you know? Because we wasn't around any.

I don't recall discussing it with my parents, but I remember that I wanted to go to Ashland the first year. And the tenth grade was not one of the ones that was integrated that year. They only integrated certain grade levels that year. And at school at that age, I guess we were really aware of the racial divide at that time. Even though we were not around white children, we had become aware that there was a white school. And we believed that we would get a

Marsha Richard school picture. Courtesy of the Richard family.

better education by goin' to the white school. We felt like we were missin' out on something that the white students were getting and that's why they didn't want us to come up there. And several of us were bound and determined that we were going to go.

My parents told us that we were going up there to get a better education. Both Mom and Dad, neither one had finished school. My mom had dropped out of fifth grade and my dad in eighth grade. And at that time, I was tenth, so I had gone further than either one of my parents. And so what to expect in high school, I don't think they really knew. But they always instilled in us that nonviolence was the best way. And so we didn't go up there really expecting to confront anyone because, you know, Mom and Dad—if we had, we had to answer to our parents when we got home.

I was lookin' forward to it. I was a little afraid that the whites might be hostile towards us. I expected to be treated really differently. I expected that I would come into some really rude teachers and some really rude students. You know, I expected the situation to be a lot worse than what it actually was when I got there.

I don't remember anything just really bad happening to me. I guess one of the worst things that happened was being in that situation the blacks were always . . . being seated at the back of the room. And I have never been a back-of-the-room person. But the negatives we handled pretty well. I remember an English teacher, and she didn't think we understood what she was sayin', but she used to call us the N-word. And she would say it in such a *proper* way that she thought that we thought she was sayin', "Negro." But she was not. And we were aware of that and there was sort of like a little . . . you know, joke with us because she thought that we didn't understand what she said. But we did. And we didn't let that bother us, and we went straight on with whatever she asked us to do.

One day we were coming from the cafeteria and there was this young white man who actually hated the fact that we were at *his* school. And whenever we would get close to him in the halls or anywhere, he would hold his nose. A bunch of us were coming from the cafeteria and he was at the west end of the building just as we were getting ready to go in. And by the time we made it to him, he grabbed that nose. And we decided that day that we were going to teach him a lesson. We made a circle around him. And we stood there. And he was standin', he was turnin' red holdin' onto that nose. And we just stood there. We didn't say one word to him. That's when he let the nose [gasps], and one of the students said, "See, it didn't hurt." Or something like that. And we walked on.

I guess they didn't think that the blacks could afford to wear some of the clothes that they wore. And I remember that we went into class one day and Joyce Gray, who was white, and Laura Dorse, who was black, showed up in class with the same identical blazer on. Joyce didn't like that. Joyce would take hers off, Laura would take hers off. Joyce would put hers on, Laura would put hers on. We were all in the back of the room and Laura was back there with us and Joyce was sitting up in the front. And it was the *funniest* thing in the world. I don't remember whether they kept them off or they kept them on, but eventually Joyce realized that whatever she did with her coat, Laura was gonna do the same thing, and she just stopped. And that went on in a teacher's classroom without the teacher even being aware of it. We looked at several things as being humorous at the time that they happened.

It was a good experience. I'm glad that I was given the opportunity to do that. And given the same situation today, I would do the same thing.

There was a time when blacks and white were separate in their thoughts and things that they worked to achieve. And today I guess they're still . . . they're separated but it's not as noticeable. Working at Walmart, I guess I use humor to handle a lot of situations. But every once in a while workin' down there a white person will come through to pay for somethin'. And when they pay you, they put the money on the counter as if not to touch your hand. And my cashiers, some of them get so angry about that. And I tell them the best way to handle the situation like that is this: When you return their change, I don't put it on the counter. I purposely put the change into their hand where my hand will purposely touch their hand. And I smile about it. I can't help but smile about it. To me, it's just so funny that they didn't wanna touch my hand. My black is not gonna rub off on them.

# Eugene and Ellie Steward

## 1927–2017 (Eugene); born 1931 (Ellie)

Interviewed December 1995 and September 2003, Michigan City, Mississippi, by Aviva Futorian, Roy DeBerry, and John Lyons

*Mr. and Mrs. Steward were both prominent activists from the very beginning. Mrs. Steward, the daughter of Charlie Reaves and niece of Henry Reaves, held the position of secretary in the Benton County Citizens Club (she is pictured, standing in front of a crowd, on this book's cover). Mrs. Steward returned to Lane College in Tennessee, where she completed her BA degree. She later worked as the director of Head Start in Benton County. As a result of his movement activities, Mr. Steward was fired as a bus driver for the school system. Later, he was elected the first black district supervisor in Benton County. Several of their children desegregated the Ashland School. The following conversation was edited from two interviews we conducted in their den.*

◆ ◆ ◆

**Ellie:** My parents separated when I was six years old. In 1938, we moved with my grandparents across where Henry Reaves lived. My mother worked for this white family, and they had a son and two daughters. We played together, climbed trees. I mean, we just kind of enjoyed each other. My mother or my dad never said, "You are black and they are white, and they are better than you are and you shouldn't have anything to do with them." We just kind of followed what she did. I was conscious of the difference, because when my mother was working, we ate what they had left. You went through the back door. Their parents wanted us to say, "Yes, ma'am" and "No, ma'am" to their children. I just said to my mother, "I hope she never asks me to do that," because her son was about the age of me. He was a young teenager, just like me. Although he was white and I was black. I said, "I'm not gonna call him no mister." She didn't say anything, because she was not going to tell me that I should say that.

**Eugene:** We always knew the difference, 'cause my mother always reminded us. She would tell a lot of things that happened to the blacks. You know, sometimes, these things grow up in you.

**Ellie:** We got married when I was seventeen and he was nineteen, maybe twenty. December 6, 1948. We had eleven kids. When we were farmers, we talked about me going back to school to become a teacher, to be able to help. My oldest sister and her husband were teachers. I just admired their way of teaching and the things that they were doing, how they were teaching the children. That's really what I wanted to be. I started in 1964 at M.I. College and I went that semester, all summer and then in the fall of '64. And a year up to the end of summer of '65. And during that time, J. D. Bennett was the superintendent of education in Benton County, and he said anybody that graduated from Rust College or Mississippi Industrial College would not get a job teaching in Benton County, because of the civil rights movement. We decided I would go to school somewhere else, so I went to Lane College in September of 1965. I went there until January 1967. And when I got home I was Head Start director. When I was hired, there were twenty-one people on the board. And the first voting, I got seventeen of the twenty-one votes to become director.

◆  ◆  ◆

**Ellie:** Uncle Henry[6] was my dad's brother, and I guess when I got big enough to know about the rights of people, he always told us about voting. When a lot of us were not doing anything, he was out there trying to get people voting and trying to get things done here for the black people. Henry Reaves was telling people to go down and register. We did. That was the time when you had to take the test. And then you had to explain this portion of the Constitution. Uncle Henry was always working on making things better. For blacks, where blacks can register to vote and . . . we just wanted things better for our children, you know?

When the civil right workers came in, there were a lot. You know, we had families that came, husbands and wives came to stay in the house with us, young people. We would ride around in the community and visit families and go to meetings, would talk about you registering to vote and going to school.

**Eugene:** I was kind of molded in it, because my mother. I really got involved when they killed Emmett Till.[7] It affected me, when they showed the picture in the paper of a . . . *kid.* When they said they drowned the boy, and he come up looking like . . . I don't know. When something happened like that, we would sit around, my brothers and I, and say, "How?" You know? "How'd this happen?" And "Why? Why would this happen to somebody?" And then we . . . [trails off]. I experienced a lot of things when we were young. I'll go back to my mother. My mother told a lot of things, what would happen. To black women and white men, and all this kind of stuff. I don't know, it just took an effect on me.

**Interviewer:** *When there was the first school integration, did all your kids choose to integrate Ashland?*

**Eugene:** I made the decision for Bobbie. She had to go, 'cause I told her. I didn't figure I should fight for something I didn't believe in myself. I know the books they was getting. When they was out of date, they would send them back to Old Salem. And I wanted my kids to have a good education. A better education than they were getting. I sat her down and we talked. And she cried. I said, "I can't help it. You got to go, Bobbie." I said, "What you think we going to the meetings for? We could get killed. I'm doing this for y'all."

She wrote me a letter when she got to North Town, Pennsylvania, after she finished college at Rust and she said, "Daddy, I never did get to tell you this. I *thank* you for sending me." I cried. I kept the letter. Ain't no telling where, but I imagine it's somewhere in a box somewhere packed up in the attic or something. But I showed it to the other kids and I said, "Look what Bobbie wrote me." Now, Chris[8] didn't know any better. Chris was in the first grade.

**Ellie:** You know what really made me mad? When Chris was going, she was the only black child on the bus going to Ashland School. I was driving to Lane College and when I'd leave on Monday morning driving to Jackson, Tennessee, sometimes she had to go up to the road to get the bus. And I would sit there and wait for the bus to come. She'd get on the bus and all those white kids—they wouldn't let her sit down. If they were on a seat, they'd sit sideways. I could see it because the bus would pull off while I was sitting there and I was so *mad.* I guess I took it out on that little Volkswagen, 'cause I drove too fast. I'd drive from my house to Jackson in less than an hour, 'cause I was so mad that they were doing Chris like that.

**Eugene:** Chris wouldn't talk about it. When she got home she wouldn't say anything about it. I think she got some hate.

Ellie Steward at a civil rights
meeting. Courtesy of Frank
Cieciorka.

Eugene Steward at a civil rights meeting.
Courtesy of Frank Cieciorka.

**Ellie:** You know, I think in a way it was worth it because it let our black children know about how the whites were and it let the whites see that everything that they said about blacks was not true. In God's eyes, it's no black and white. In God's eyes. I don't think all whites should be put in the same barrel and I don't think all blacks should be. For almost thirty years, I worked with whites in Head Start, and I've worked with some of the worst of 'em, and I've worked with some of the best of 'em. And, you know, once you get together, our people say, you know, white folk is this and all black look alike. That is not true. But to me it was good for all the children, for school integration, and they all got the same education. I think it was good.

# Barbara "Bobbie" Steward-Hardaway

## Born 1952

Interviewed November 2014, Michigan City, Mississippi, by Aviva Futorian, Roy DeBerry, and John Lyons

*One of eleven children of Eugene and Ellie Steward, Ms. Steward-Hardaway desegregated Ashland her freshman year of high school. At the time, she was vehemently opposed to leaving Old Salem, the all-black school, but her parents insisted. It was a decision she'd later thank them for. She sat down with us in her parents' living room.*

◆ ◆ ◆

I had ten siblings, eleven kids including myself, and I was the third from the eldest. My parents lived on a farm, their own land. We always worked our own land. We had all kinds of fields surrounding us. Seems like we were always working in cotton fields, corn fields, pea fields, cucumber fields, some kind of fields. We were always working no matter what time of year it was, we were always working. My dad worked us very hard, which I don't have any regrets about it. It made me the person I am today.

When I was growing up that's all we knew—white people and black people. We didn't know all of other nationalities. But I always knew that there was difference. It always, forever all my life, seemed as if the Caucasians were more privileged. They could do things that we as blacks could not do. And we always had to address people as "Yes, ma'am, no, ma'am" or "Miss" or "Missus" whatever. They were allowed to call us whatever they wanted to call us. Really until the school integration started in Benton County, it didn't mean much to me. We never really ate out, so we didn't go in the restaurants. When I left Old Salem

School after eighth grade and started school at Ashland High in ninth grade is when everything really started coming into being. I really started seeing the difference and realizing what color really meant.

School integration started out by choice, by grades. When I finished eighth grade, it was to the point where I could choose if I wanted to stay at Old Salem, which was the all-black school, or go to Ashland High, which was the all-white school. Of course, I wanted to stay where I was. But I wasn't doing so very well in school because I just wanted to do other things with my friends and not concentrate on my studies. My dad made me go to Ashland School. He made me go to a different school. And I thank him for doing that today because if he had not, I wouldn't even know if I'd have finished high school. I was headed down that road pretty much.

I remember going to Ashland High School on the first day, everybody going into the gym. Somewhat apprehensive, probably nervous, a little afraid because this was it. I'd never been in a world where I had to be this close in dealing with Caucasians. My mom has always taught us: "Don't be afraid of no one. You're no better than anybody else, but you're no less than anybody else, regardless of your skin color. Don't be afraid, you have every right that they have. You are just as much as they are."

It was not a whole lot of blacks there at the time. So we all kind of bonded together. That's when I really started feeling the racism. Seeing it openly. You get on the bus, and a seat might have one person on it, they'd sit on the edge of the seat so you couldn't sit down. Or being called the N-word many times. Many times I've been called that word. You walked on the sidewalks at school during breaks or whatever and they would try to force you off the sidewalk. Most of the times, we just stood our ground. There were times when we would just step off the sidewalk. There are times that I have done that.

I remember that I had to work very hard to pass. I had to do over and above what the average white kid had to do in order to pass. I had to work very hard. The requirements, the discipline at the former all-black school was not the same as it was there. And on my part, I hadn't paid much attention to my last couple of years, my junior high years. But I did pretty well. I was determined that I wasn't going to fail. It was the beginning of me learning how to interact and it helped me to prepare for the outer world. Because, you know, there's a lot of racism out there. Because I had that experience that I had got to Ashland High School, it really prepared me for the outside world. And it also taught me that to succeed, I have to have a high expectation of myself and a high self-esteem, I had to think and believe that I can do anything anybody could do regardless of what it takes. For sure, it was worth it.

**Interviewer:** *What was the most surprising thing in your encounters with other white students?*

There were some nice ones as well as not so nice ones. That was probably the most surprising. I mean, as a young person that age, you just always think that they're all the same. And I'm sure they probably felt the same way about us. That we were all the same.

# Crystal Steward

## Born 1959

Interviewed September 2003, outside of Ashland, Mississippi, by Aviva Futorian, Roy DeBerry, and John Lyons

*All of seven years old, Ms. Steward was among the three black students who desegregated Ashland Elementary's first grade in 1967. The experience was traumatic. As opposed to some older black students, she didn't understand why she was forced to desegregate, or even what that meant. One of eleven children born to Ellie and Eugene Steward, she now works two jobs in Jackson, Tennessee, at a grocery store and a bottling company. We spoke to her in the home of her uncle, Henry Reaves.*

◆ ◆ ◆

I don't think I knew I was integrating a white school. We integrated Ashland Elementary School, and there was only three blacks at that time—Naomi Reaves,[9] Thurman Rose, and myself.

My parents had explained to us what was going on—that we was gonna go to an all-white school and it would be different. We would be treated differently but just go ahead anyway, just go to school, try to learn.

When me and Thurman got on the bus, children would move away. To my recollection, they had us on the front seat of the bus. We had to sit on the front seat. You know, we wouldn't, couldn't, go back and sit. When we got on the bus the white kids moved back. We would hear them talking, calling us names. They would blow spitballs all the time at us and call us niggers. We'd be on the sidewalk walking, and when they would see us coming, they would shove us off the sidewalk. We'd have to get off the sidewalk 'cause we saw them coming. We would just get off the sidewalk and keep walking. I think it was more so because we was afraid. We were the only three there so I think we were more afraid because when something would happen, they would all go huddle up together. And there was only three of us.

I can't really remember what it was that happened that we got put out of the class, all three of us. It was something to do with Thurman. He got into it with one of the kids in the classroom and the class erupted. Naomi came to his aid more so than I did because Naomi was like her mom and dad. She had *power* behind her. She was really forceful and very outspoken at the time, even being a young girl like she was. She looked out for Thurman, and when all was said and done we all three got put out of the classroom that day. I remember thinking, "We don't have to come back here. We won't have to come back here the next day." And I remember Mother and Daddy telling us, "Well, you're going back." I remember not wanting to be in the classroom. "Why?" You know? Even then the white kids was asking, "Why are we there?" I would go home every day hoping I didn't have to go back the next day. I'm sure I said something to Mother because I'd always talk to Mother, you know. And then some things, you didn't say what happened because there was so much.

Me and Naomi used to talk a lot about things that happened. We used to cry all the time. Together—in school, out of school. Here, in this very house. In the bedroom, we would be in there crying about how we didn't want to go back. But we knew we had to because we knew our parents and Henry and Ginevera was *determined*. And you couldn't understand back then why. We were just little children.

I think about Naomi a lot. Before Naomi died, she was twelve, along the way is when we really realized what was going on. And I think about the times that we went through and things . . . we saw a lot. Daddy and Mother was very much so involved in civil rights. Uncle Henry used to take us around to the marches and the meetings. We would see things that we couldn't understand. And me and Naomi would be sitting there at meetings. I remember once we looked at each other and said, "Why are we here? Why are we stayin'?" We'd be wishing they'd hurry up and come on, not knowing that . . . that they were really there for *us*.

◆ ◆ ◆

When I got into ninth grade, I played ball at Ashland. At that time they didn't care, they just wanted to win, you know. It was like a win-win situation with them. They had white and black on the team. But we was still segregated: You had a white "Most Beautiful" in school, you had a black "Most Beautiful." You had a white "Most Likely to Succeed," and you had a black "Most Likely to

Crystal Steward school picture.
Courtesy of the Benton County
Historical Society.

Succeed." And I think that stopped when we got like in the eleventh grade. It took ten years.

I suppressed a lot of memories to be able to move on with my life. In order to be able to deal with the world, to make it in the world, you had to. I came out with some hatred. Because I'd always felt that whites had it better than we did, and it was easier. And even now it's easier for them, you know what I'm sayin'? To advance, to succeed. I see it every day where I'm at now. Even working now at the grocery store. You have whites walk up, and they see you standing there with no customers in your line and they'll walk right on past you and get in a line, a long line with a white cashier. I don't think it has made me bitter. Because I can tell the difference when a person's really *real.* And I think the reason why it doesn't make me as angry as it probably could have, is because of Mother. Because Mother always instilled in us, all eleven of us children, you treat people the way you want to be treated. You do not discriminate because of the color of skin.

It's easy to think back and hate people for what they did. And it's easy to blame everybody else for what the white people did to us back then. And you can easily get off on blaming people today. And you have to tell yourself, "Lord, help me to look past that." And, you know, it all boils down to right now my life is getting to heaven, seeing God for myself. In order to get to heaven, I have to love everybody, I have to love everybody as God loves me.

I haven't seen a lot of my classmates in a long time. But when I've seen them I've been glad to see them. Because before I graduated I had a lot of white classmates that was really nice. I've had two classmates that would always find themselves apologizing. Like, "My parents were like this but this is not the way I am," you know.

**Interviewer:** *If you had kids, would you have any hesitation about sending them into a situation like yours?*

I would not have any hesitation. The explanation I would give to them is to better life for themselves as well as the future of our children. Then they'd have an open field to see. You learn to mingle and you learn to *love*. Because in this world today you're going to have to deal with white and black. It's an open thing. And you can't do this "Well, I don't want to do this because there's white people over here," or "I don't want to do this because there's black people over there." Some kind of way you gonna have to entwine, you gonna have to come together. 'Cause that's the only way we're gonna make it.

It was all worth it. Even though things are not the way they really should be now, they're a lot better. We're not where we ought to be, but thank the Lord, we're not where we used to be.

# The Tiplers

## 1907–2004 (Clee Anna), 1927–2014 (Albert), 1928–2010 (Nelma)

Interviewed December 1995, Lamar, Mississippi, by Aviva Futorian, Roy DeBerry, and Wilbur Colom

*Nelma and Albert Tipler were two of the most active citizens in the Benton County movement, some of which they attributed to owning their own land. "Sharecroppers or people who lived on people's places, they wanted to be in the meetings, but they knowed better to try because they could be put off the land," Nelma explained. They had fourteen children, some of whom desegregated Ashland. Their daughter Alberta worked on the* Benton County Freedom Train *newsletter, and managed the Citizens Club office in 1965 before going to college at the University of Wisconsin and law school at Rutgers University. They were joined in this conversation by Clee Anna Tipler Richards, Albert's mother, who housed white SNCC volunteers in her home.*

◆ ◆ ◆

**Nelma:** Autumn of 1965, the white people were like a train. They would wait till about ten o'clock at night. They would come from Ashland, seventeen or eighteen cars. They would come straight up this road [Hudsonville Road] and turn there [Hoover Road] at the Freedom House.[10] And they would go on around there and blow their horns. I don't know why they did it, but I would be a little bit afraid. I didn't know if they was gonna shoot or something or what. One night I was in the bed. This was in the fall of 1965. They tried to firebomb the Freedom House. I got up and looked out the window. And when I looked out, a car was pulling away from the blaze. I don't know if I heard the car and that woke me up, but me and Albert went down there and we put that fire out. Wasn't damage done no more than knocked the window out.

And they burned a cross, down there at the office, right next to the house. And you know the Byrds[11] shot in our yard? One evening Dexter[12] was toting in wood, and they shot in the yard out there. Now that's when I got scared. I was scared they would hurt my children, and after they did that I was really scared.

The men had guns but they didn't get up and get them, 'cause they was taught to be nonviolent. But now, after they shot in the yard, Albert got his. We were waiting for 'em to come back. We wouldn't have gotten them all, but we would have gotten some.

**Albert:** I think when something like this taking place, the people that's involved in it, you can't help but be frightened. Emmett Till was visiting his grandparents in Tallahatchie County, and he was taken out the home, at night, and they found him in the creek somewhere.

**Nelma:** Now I worried about it because I thought about all them boys that I had. I had seven boys and seven girls. And I worried about something like that. But then I said, "Maybe this will help them," when we was working with the civil rights, and we would go to vote, elect who we tried to elect. And it has helped some.

**Albert:** What it really was about was making things better and more equal for everybody.

Daddy always told us, "You don't have full citizenship to act in nothing unless you're a registered voter." So Mr. Henry Reaves had this voter registration drive on. He got me really interested and he give me a sample ballot. Said, "You promise you go to Ashland next week and register." I said, "I'll go."

**Nelma:** They was a little frightened about going to vote after being registered. 'Cause it was nobody but just all whites would be at the poll. Some of them was kind of hesitant to go. But they went. When we went up and tried to register, they would give you all these hard constitutional questions, which we had never seen and didn't understand.

**Clee Anna:** I sure tried. When I went to register, there were so many questions they had on it, I just missed them. I didn't pass. I know I went three times.

**Nelma:** I remember when they built the Citizens Club office down there. And they put out a paper every week.[13] We would write little pieces and the people would bring 'em. I'd take it to her,[14] and she would type up the paper and sometimes I would run it off. We take them around to folk's homes and then we'd

Nelma Tipler. Courtesy of Frank Cieciorka.

take them to meetings. You know, we always take a big stack to the meetings. Teaster Baird would pick up so many. Spence Richard would pick up some. And A. Z. Smith would pick 'em up. Remember y'all used to fix those little flyers and go around and give 'em out? And that would make people come to the meetings and see y'all would talk and what you had to say sounded good. That things was gonna be better for us. Greenwood is my church, but I went to all the meetings wherever they met.

**Interviewer:** *When Don Jelinek* [a white lawyer from New York] *stayed at your house, were you frightened?*

**Clee Anna:** Well, I was frightened a little when the Klan come through. See, they come through there two nights and there was about six or seven cars, may been more than that. When they got going around the cars, they went to shooting.

**Nelma:** Yeah, Don wanted his bed moved to a different window. He was scared.

**Interviewer:** *After all of these years do you think it was worth being involved?*

**Clee Anna:** Sure, it was worth it. We'll enjoy some other day the results from that. My great-grandchildren are having a better time than the children had because it's better for them. Because if you hadn't come and started this like it is now, they wouldn't have had that chance. They would have probably been on the shovel somewhere.

**Nelma:** Before the movement, it was tough. Before we moved, and Mama and Daddy give us the acre of land to put our first old house on, we worked for a while as sharecroppers. Me and Albert with all the children. It was tough. I went to the field, although I was pregnant, and things was tough. You might make a crop. If you didn't figure with the man, you didn't get nothing out of it. How many years did we stay there? Eight years. Some few of those eight years we didn't get nothing. But the most of 'em we cleared something out of our crop.

I just prayed about it and stayed on in it. Because if you go to the Lord for the right thing, He'll guide. And see, it just got on my mind to stay in it.

# Dexter and Gaither Tipler

## Born 1957 (Gaither) and 1959 (Dexter)

Interviewed September 2003, Lamar, Mississippi, by Aviva Futorian and John Lyons

*Dexter and Gaither are the sons of Albert and Nelma Tipler. They desegregated Ashland Elementary School in the first and third grades, respectively. Sitting in the front yard of their parents' house, they talked about the chaos leading up to the movement and what they were able to understand of the situation at the time, given their young ages.*

◆ ◆ ◆

**Gaither:** One day we was getting wood—Dexter and Alvin[15] and myself. Some cars came up, stopped, and all we heard was the shooting. And quite naturally the first thing we did, we ran in the house. The car shot on off. Being older than Dexter and Alvin, I kind of knew what was going on . . . you know, white folks felt like we were trying to gain our freedom.

**Dexter:** I can't recall what my mom and dad said. But I can recall that we knew we was integrating the schools and that there would be problems. It was not so much that I knew what was going on. I knew what was going on around me. I knew what I was taught, and I knew from up from when they started the *Freedom Train* newspaper and things. I knew from hearing older people talk. Not that, as in being as young as I was, I *understood*. I just knew that by him being white, he could do what he wanted, and I could do what he say.

**Gaither:** People talk, okay? I feel like I comprehend pretty well. I heard Momma and Daddy talk. So when you integrate a school, they can't tell you what's going to happen exactly. But they're gonna tell you it's gonna be some problems. They could've told me then, "It could be racist." I didn't know what racist meant then. "What is that?" They didn't tell us "racist," but they did tell us there was gonna be problems.

**Dexter:** You can understand it because, see basically, you can know they don't want you to know. There'd be things that Mommy and Daddy talked about that they didn't want us to hear. But you know how it goes.

**Gaither:** And you could hear them, and quite naturally they didn't want us to know about the fear. But I knew they was, because I hear good. They were brave for their kids. But I could tell even though they're brave, they're scared too.

We were never shot at again, but they burned crosses, you know. I really didn't understand what the sense was in burning a cross. I really didn't even know what a cross was then. All I knew was Momma saying, "Those white folks." Daddy usually sharecropped for Ku Klux Klansmen, too. Then one time there was a line of them that came down here and they came past the Freedom House, and turned and came down this way. If I'm not mistaken, they didn't shoot at nobody, but did shoot when they got around the corner. About fifteen, twenty cars. It was just about dark then, and they all came down this way. Folks that we would sharecrop with was in that bunch.

I remember the first day of school. The teachers, they was nice in their way, but they made sure they separated what few blacks there were, they'd put in the back of the classroom, on the same side. There were probably only four or five of us in that same room then. Even though some went out of their way to be nice to you, you could tell that you really weren't wanted somewhere.

**Dexter:** School wasn't the problem. It was after I got on the bus. We had a guy driving the bus, he's now highway patrolman. We'd get on the bus, even then, he wanted the blacks to sit on one side, further to the back, together. Because the bus would be cold, the heat should get on the white folks.

**Interviewer:** *Did you make friends with white kids?*

**Gaither:** Yeah, because I had a big mouth. I always did make friends. Whether you want to be my friend or not, you're going to talk to me. But there's going to be some taught differently.

**Dexter:** Some was just taught not to make friends with you. It was almost as if when a problem arose with white students it's because, "You shouldn't talk to that nigger." That was just the way it was.

Dexter Tipler school picture. Courtesy of the        Gaither Tipler school picture. Courtesy of
Benton County Historical Society.                    the Benton County Historical Society.

**Gaither:** It didn't really get better. All the white folks left the school and went out of the county to another school. So you can't say it got better.

**Interviewer:** *What was the best part of integrating?*

**Dexter:** Me and you sitting, talking now. I don't have to worry about, "Is someone coming to the house tonight because I was talking to a white lady?" I've been a few places in my life. I've been to California, to Maine, to Chicago and Indiana, and some other places. You are as likely to see a black man and a white woman anywhere you go now. Back then, you weren't allowed to be seen.

**Interviewer:** *Would you do it again?*

**Gaither:** Yes, in a heartbeat. After it started, I probably would have told you no. But seeing how things have changed, I would do again. Why? Because I think not only did black folks learn a lesson, but white folks did, too. That we *had* to get along. Benton County didn't belong to them.

# Chapter 3

# SIBLINGS

*In addition to talking with multiple generations of the same families, we also talked with several siblings, sometimes at once. Coming of age during the movement often meant being on the front lines—most commonly among those who desegregated the school. In an increasingly difficult and turbulent world, these siblings turned to each other for strength, courage, and inspiration.*

# The Dorses

## 1947 (Philips), 1948–2019 (Jo Ann), 1949 (Rebecca), 1951 (Lloyd), 1953 (Jeanette)

Interviewed August 2007, Memphis, Tennessee, by Aviva Futorian, Roy DeBerry, John Lyons, and Stephen Klein

*Lloyd, Jeanette, Jo Ann, Philips, and Rebecca Dorse were among the eleven children of Joe and Rebecca Dorse, two very active members of the movement. They were not sharecroppers but instead rented land from Ms. Hamer, a white woman, until their civil rights activities caused her to raise their rent and forced them off the land. Jo Ann and Rebecca were among the first class of school desegregators at the Ashland School in 1965. They were an incredibly close-knit family during the movement and remain so today. The following conversation took place around a dining room table in the home of Philips, in Memphis.*

◆ ◆ ◆

**Jo Ann:** Our parents were farmers. We were not sharecroppers, we were renters.

**Philips:** From Ms. Hamer, a white lady. We was renting from her for four bales of cotton a year. When we picked cotton, we made like fifteen bales a year. The first four bales, the best four bales, she automatically got.

**Jo Ann:** My parents were the parents of eleven children. One died as a baby, and it was six girls and four boys. We farmed, but our main source of income was cotton. We raised our own food. From okra fields to watermelons, sweet potatoes, cows, pigs, chickens.

**Rebecca:** When you live on the farm, every morning you get up early, just about daybreak. Usually your mother has been in the kitchen and cooked breakfast.

**Jo Ann:** Everybody, from the time you were big enough to have a pillowcase, they would put holes in each side for handles. If you were four years old, you were in the fields picking cotton.

**Philips:** We'd go work in the field by 6 a.m.; we stop and come home at 11:30 [for lunch].

**Rebecca:** We worked to almost sundown. We talked about picking cotton, but you also chop cotton. You're trying to get rid of the grass and the weeds so the cotton would grow and multiply. The dirt would be hot on your feet. Your hands would get sore. And guess what? You kept on going. If it was cloudy, we would pray for rain because we felt like, "Oh, I'm so sick of this. Always so hot."

◆ ◆ ◆

**Jo Ann:** My first awareness of racism, I suppose was that our churches were totally black. Schools were totally black. And Caucasian kids didn't go to school with us, so I knew there was a difference.

**Rebecca:** I remember once we went to Holly Springs. I guess I was seven or eight years old, and our mother took us to the courthouse. We had to use the bathroom and it had signs that wrote "colored" and "white." We were always at home and in our little comfort zone. This was when I kind of knew there was a difference. And then, when someone who was white came near us, our mother would always stand back. And I thought, "Why is she doing that?" If you don't get and go out into the public, you don't realize all these things exist because when you're at home, everything is nice. You're happy, you know? You might not have that many material things, but at least you are happy. And you're loved.

**Philips:** From our house, we had to walk miles to school; it would take about an hour and a half or two hours. And the white kids rode the bus. I was wondering why they were riding the bus, and we had to walk in the rain or cold or whatever. And when we'd see the bus come, we'd get over because they would throw stuff out the bus at us. And a white girl who had a job, Shirley Miller, at the Cotton Patch Café, we would see her, and would speak to her across the fence. But whenever she went to work, she would work inside, serving the whites. But we had to go to the side window that served blacks only. They didn't allow blacks to go in the building. The only blacks they allowed in the building would work in the kitchen. They would serve us from the window, but we couldn't go inside the building.

**Jo Ann:** We were excited when civil rights workers came around and we went to the meetings at night. They would speak about change that was coming in the schools and the restaurants and different things, it was really exciting. I thought it was great. "Lord, here comes some help!"

**Rebecca:** I was so happy. The civil rights movement in Benton County got us together. All of us would meet at the church. We would go from church to church, and we were singing. We saw our parents up front. Some of the leaders—Mr. Henry Reaves, Ms. Steward was secretary. Our mother was the assistant secretary. And there we were, singing these good songs. We'd hold hands and rock and sing, "Oh, Freedom!" Being a kid, oh, our hearts were into that and we felt so good.

**Philips:** "We Shall Overcome." And it would be just like church service. Everybody around the community would be there, but for two or three hours, and get together.

**Jo Ann:** And we'd start doing the newspaper down in Holly Springs.

**Rebecca:** Oh, the *Benton County Freedom Train*. We couldn't wait to get the paper to read to see what was in it.

**Jo Ann:** We'd go in different places and marches. In Holly Springs. And Jackson, Mississippi. Mr. Henry Reaves took us to that voter registration march in June of 1965. Some individuals from Benton County went down. My sister, Lloyd, and myself, were part of that. While we were in Jackson, we marched and we were arrested.

**Rebecca:** When I woke up the next morning, Jo Ann and Lloyd were not at home. I said, "Where is Jo Ann and Lloyd?" My mother said, "They went to Jackson to go to jail."

**Jo Ann:** We were little girls. I was about sixteen and Lloyd was probably fourteen. We were arrested in Jackson, and we were herded off like cattle to the fairgrounds. And we were there at least three or four nights.

**Lloyd:** We were put in the back of a police paddy wagon. There was no air in that thing, we were packed in like sardines. They would drive fast and hit the brakes and throw us. At the fairgrounds, we were in a big old barn; at night the older ladies were like our guardians. There was a lot of young people in there, the older ladies would stay up all night to watch over us.

**Jo Ann:** They had guards guarding us of course, white guards. They talked bad to us. I saw some ugly things that went on. Some of the older black women, stepping out having sex with the guards to get special favors. I never forgot that. Mr. Reaves came down there to get us. He sympathized with us. And he was the responsible adult to pick us up and bring us back home to our parents. They asked us what happened and we told them. But, of course, I didn't tell them about that thing about the women. We just told them everything else, and they were glad we were back safe. They were all right with it because they knew this is something you have to go through to get your rights. Somebody has to do it. Everybody can't sit back and say, "I'm not going. My children can't get put in jail." Or "I might get knocked down." Somebody has to *stand* for something. That's the old saying, "If you don't stand for something, you'll fall for anything."

**Lloyd:** My parents had a lot of faith in us. I was so glad to go home because being down there . . . my parents weren't there and my sister Jo Ann and I were the only two in my family that was there. It was really an experience.

◆ ◆ ◆

**Jo Ann:** My mother was always into school. She taught her mother how to read and write. And she wanted us to do better. She didn't want her daughters standing up, sweating over nobody's stove and cleaning nobody's house. She was always a very positive person, and my dad was right there with her.

**Lloyd:** I remember when she went to the March on Washington in 1963. She had ten children at home and left all of us alone with Daddy. Daddy was a cook in the navy, World War II. That's where I get my name Lloyd from. He named me after some guy in the navy. But my daddy was a cook in the navy, so he was able to cook and feed all of us, while my mom was gone.

**Rebecca:** I was so happy that he supported her and allowed her to go that far away from home to participate in civil rights, I thought that was really admirable.

◆ ◆ ◆

**Jo Ann:** Our parents wanted better schooling for us. And we knew the white school had better books than the black school did. They had better . . . everything. We were excited to be integrating. Our parents was all for it, and they had three children that integrated three grades—twelfth, eleventh, and first grade. So my parents had more children going to the white school the first year than any family in Benton County. And we were just excited to be going because we were looking for better than we had at Old Salem.

**Rebecca:** I hated to leave my friends at Old Salem High. I liked the people at Old Salem, but if this is what our parents told us to do because this is supposed to help us in the future, so be it. We were told, "Now, when you all go to the school, whatever the white kids say to you, don't say anything back, keep your mouth shut and just go to school." We didn't think they'd call us all those names. *All* those names.

**Jo Ann:** Of course they didn't want us there. I mean, we're the fly in the buttermilk. We knew that. Our white neighbors—two long blocks up the road, we used to pick cotton and chop cotton with them. They did the same work we did. Didn't have air conditioning, just like we didn't. They were poorer than we were. And when we rode the bus with them, they had the *audacity* to call us the N-word. We would sit on the front of the bus near the bus driver as close as possible, and they would sit at the back of the bus, take a sheet of paper and then spit in it, ball it up and throw it at the back of our heads. When we'd look back, they would be looking down. And everybody'd swear nobody did it. As long as we were working for them or with them, we were okay. But once we went to school with them, they thought they were better than we were.

**Rebecca:** It was just a few of us that went that first year in 1965. We were like family because the white kids they wouldn't even talk to us.

**Jo Ann:** We needed that bond.

**Rebecca:** We did not know that our names will come out in the *Southern Advocate*.[1] And somebody brought the paper to a civil rights meeting, and the parents, the black parents, were so proud of us, because we had made honor roll. So they left you with some hope. That just because you went to a Caucasian school, we as black people were just as smart as white people.

**Interviewer:** *Why did the family leave Mississippi in 1966?*

**Rebecca:** Ms. Hamer had relatives out there in the county and some of them might not have liked the idea that our mother and father was so active in civil

Jo Ann Dorse school picture.
Courtesy of the Benton County
Historical Society.

rights. And that some of their children attended Ashland High, so that might have been a way for her to get rid of us, force us to move.

**Philips:** Our rent went up to five bales of cotton. Integration, fooling with the freedom movement. And everybody black that rented from Ms. Hamer in Benton County, she went up a bale on everybody. We were paying four bales, she went up to five. We were broke, didn't have nothing. We stayed on that farm about twenty years. Everything we had you could put it in a station wagon or the back of a truck. And nine children. Now I was working in the city [Memphis], I would go out there every weekend and buy them groceries. So, it wasn't no sense in them staying in the country, and I had to drive fifty miles every week to buy groceries and stuff. So I said, "Move in the city and we'll buy a home." And he's still in the same home forty-something some years.

◆ ◆ ◆

**Interviewer:** *Tell us about your high school reunion.*

**Rebecca:** Twenty-five years after 1967, it would have been 1992. Philips called me and said, "Rebecca, some white lady called my house, wanted your phone number." And when he gave me her name, right away I remembered—Deborah Bruce. She was really smart in school. I called her and she said, "Rebecca, we are interested in having a class reunion, and would you like to participate?" I said, "Well, you know, Deborah, I didn't graduate with you all because we moved." She

said, "I know, but you went to school with us and you're still part of our class."
And she said, "We would really love to have you." Loyal Thompson and I were
the only black students who showed up at the reunion. Loyal had a date and I
was by myself. So, at the reunion, they kind of indirectly apologized. I forgot
how they did it, but it was kind of came across like they were sorry about what
happened when we went to Ashland High. It just blew my mind, just blew me
away. When I first got there, they were walking up to me, hugging me. I think
they did that so I would feel comfortable, welcome. So I would continue to
participate and they were very concerned about what I was doing, where have
I been, where do I live, you know, all that kind of stuff. And I thought, "What
is happening?" I'm kind of looking around, "Am I in the right place?"

**Jo Ann:** I see now from being raised out in the country, like a lot of them were
raised out there. They have never been nowhere but Ashland and Hickory Flat
or Greenwood, Mississippi. They'd never been anywhere. But people that have
been places and lived places, they know it's a whole other world out there.

**Rebecca:** And then I think some of the classmates came to the realization: It's
not a white world. It's the world of all people and it takes all of us in the mix
to get the job done and to live and get along.

◆ ◆ ◆

**Philips:** My mother's dream was she wanted her children to make a living with a
pencil. So, we are blessed, we all make a living with a pencil. Nobody works in a field.

**Rebecca:** As we got older, we saw that working on the farm, you really couldn't
have that much. Can you imagine a family of ten kids and a mother and a
father living in a house, only had two bedrooms, a hallway, a kitchen, and a
front porch? That's how we lived.

**Jo Ann:** We had four full-sized beds, so in each bed it would be two people at
the top of the bed and one at the bottom in the middle. And their feet would
be stuck in your mouth or your eye [laughter].

**Rebecca:** They inspired us to want to do better.

**Jo Ann:** Daddy wanted his children to live much better than he lived—

**Jeanette:** And we made it.

# Rosa Evans

## Born 1956

Interviewed September 2013, Ashland, Mississippi, by Aviva Futorian, Roy DeBerry, and John Lyons

*The daughter of civil rights leader Charlie Reaves, and the niece of Henry Reaves, Ms. Reaves desegregated the Ashland School in 1966, a year after the first black students arrived. The process of desegregation was staggered by grade, so when she attended fifth grade in the fall of 1966, she, along with her cousin, were the first black students in their grade. She spoke with us in the front yard of her family home, built by her father in 1964, where she's a full time caregiver for her sister Janice.*

◆ ◆ ◆

The property we're sitting on now is inherited. My father, Charlie Reaves, bought this property from his other siblings. I know that his father as a black man had a business and his name was Levi Reaves. I'm not sure exactly what it was, but it had something to do with a sawmill or something like that. Somehow he was swindled out of it by white people. I don't know how old my grandfather was when he died, but from what I hear from older people, he was an outstanding, upstanding man.

I know that to own land, that gave you a sense of power. Because most people were sharecroppers and they had to answer to someone else. We worked hard so my dad could keep what he had. And he made that known to us. You know, "This is mine. I worked hard for this." He struggled. I think he was forty-five years old before he even attended college. Because he couldn't as a black man. So he learned. My father was a carpenter/contractor. This house, he built from the ground in 1964. This is a solid house. It's a solid foundation. What he did—he put himself into it. He put all he had into it. And he worked and strived to be the best at what he did.

He was a fighter. Lived to be ninety-two years old, standing. He believed in doing what was right. My mother taught us values, morals. Being a Reaves is like being a child of Martin Luther King, because my dad stood for something. He taught us that standing for what's right will carry you further than anything you could do wrong. The Reaves name in Benton County is strong. Now, when I go into places of business and I say I'm Charlie Reaves's daughter, I get a great reception. "Your dad was a good man. Your dad was an outstanding man." And that means a lot to me. I know that he wasn't afraid. He knew his place. He knew how far to go. He knew when to walk away and when to put up a fight. All those things I look at now, and I see the person who he was in what he fought for, and why he fought for it. And there was not a lot of followers of the movement, but he paved the way for so many others.

◆ ◆ ◆

My fifth-grade year, that's when the integrating of schools started. And our father had us attend Ashland. Our second cousin, Walter Reaves's daughter, Mary Jane, was in fifth grade with me. On days when she didn't attend school, I was the only black in the class. It was very . . . I would have to say that looking back, it was very difficult. Having to deal with all these other things that were going on. The hatred. The name-calling. I didn't know the intent of the hatred when I was in the classroom at the time. There were times in the lunchroom where we had to be the last one in line to be served. Most of the time we sat together, all the blacks sat together. There was no activities . . . you were never part of the class. You were just there.

As a fifth grader, I really didn't understand. I had gone to lots of meetings with my dad, and my uncles and cousins. We had attended meetings about what was going on, how there was discrimination. I knew that the fight was to allow blacks to step forward and be recognized. I understood that, being around and listening to my dad talk. But I did not understand the intent, or the depth of the hatred. In fifth grade, there's not a lot of things you understand. I wanted to be back in the classroom,[2] where it was fun and we could sit outside and play. Recess [in Ashland] was more like, "Why am I here? Why I am doing this?"

I saw teachers feed into the negativity. They were just as racist as the students. We used to play this game at the end of the day called 7 Up. And that day my cousin was not in class. There were a few white students that tried to be cordial and play the part. The game was you put your head on your desk and someone touches you on the head, there was seven people standing up, and you tried to guess the person that touched you. I got to stand up, and I remember touching this white student on the head so she could guess who I was. And she guessed who I was, so that meant I sat down. When she stood up, she wiped the back of her hair as if I given her some type of disease. And the teacher looked at her and [nods], went along with it as if to say, "Yeah. Do that." I looked at it, and it just showed me a different . . . it made me look at the teacher different. It didn't make me step back, but it made me see the real person she was.

We had a spelling bee. And I out-spelled anyone in my class. Once you won your class, you had to go in front of the whole auditorium, and spell before the whole elementary school. And when I spelled a word, you would think you'd receive a great reception. You'd be cheered on. But when I spelled a word correctly, I was booed in an auditorium of three or four hundred students. It was like the whole auditorium. Oh my goodness. Me being the only black person that excelled that far in spelling, there was so much tension there. And the more I spelled and the closer I got to becoming the finalist, the more tension there was in there.

To this day, I haven't forgotten the word I misspelled. A simple word that I could spell backwards. But because of the tension that was there, I misspelled "popcorn." When I misspelled that word, the whole auditorium stood up and was like a standing ovation, "I'm so glad she's out of this contest." It was like, I felt . . . I can't really put it into words. That was the first experience that I had really, of how strong hate could be. I wanted to go to Jackson and be in the contest, but I lost focus because of the tension that was in the room. And to this day, that has taught me a lot. To not be focused on the negative but to stand for the positive. It has helped me in a lot of situations, to overcome.

◆ ◆ ◆

After Ashland, I got married, moved to Chicago. I worked at the Ford Motor Company, I worked in a few clothing stores. Just kind of kicked back and looked at how people were living there. Cost of living was high, and I just didn't like the atmosphere. It was a cold city with a lot of cold people. I couldn't blend in with the lifestyle there. I do feel that in Chicago, racism is a strong thing.

I moved back after fourteen years. I appreciate the peace here. I've moved back to the home house. I'm a caregiver for my sister. I find comfort in giving back what was given to me. Caring for my mother. Caring for my sister.

**Interviewer:** *Do you think things have changed from when you were in fifth grade, in terms of black people and white people?*

Rosa Evans. Courtesy of the Benton County Historical Society.

Charlie Reaves. Courtesy of the Reaves family.

I want to put this in the best words I can. I think they deal with us because they have to. I think some white people have grown past that. But some of the them still cover it up, to an extent. I can certainly look past it now, because I know it's total ignorance. I can sell myself to anybody—white, black, whatever color. I can get past that. Just four or five months ago, the gentleman that lives at the end of the road, I had his son working on a computer for me. And I called for his son. And his son wasn't in. He says, "He won't be back in till later on tonight. You can call back later, just leave a message." And he knows me, knows my mom, knows my dad. We go past that house every time we leave. And he said just call him back later on tonight or tomorrow. So I called back. And he answered the phone, and I asked for his son. And he didn't know that he had pushed the button so I could hear. And he took the phone to his son, and son asked him who is it. And he said, "Nigger woman that lives down the road." And at first something began to boil up inside and I felt like I was gonna go up there and tell him, "I'm not no nigger woman!" Who does he think he is? But then I said, "No." I could look past it. I could look past it. I know when they're sitting around talking, when they're having dinner, they still consider us niggers. They don't say it. When they're angry, I'm a nigger. A nigger woman. But I can look at them and say, "No. I'm not. I'm a black woman, and you're the one who's acting more like a nigger than me." So I can look past it now, I've outgrown it.

As I look back now, I really appreciate it. That my father wanted us to go there [Ashland] and be a part of this. As I got older, I started to understand why it was so important to try and break the ice.

I'm fifty-seven years old now, and I can still feel . . . the strength of the hatred, how strong it was at the time. And you realized you were there at school only because you were fighting, not because you were wanted or appreciated. I could say that it made it hard. But I don't want to say that. I want to say it made *me* hard. It made me tougher. It helped me be the woman I am today. Strong. Determined. A fighter, never willing to give up. I can appreciate what I went through now. At the time, I didn't. At the time I felt like it was a punishment. Now I realize, through education and through life, that it was really a fight worth fighting. I feel good that I was one of the people that fought. That sat in the classroom. That stood up for others. My father, I was more afraid of him than I was of anybody in the classroom. He stressed the fact that he wanted me to do good. He believed that I could do good. Hearing that from him built something inside of me. That I knew I had to stand up and fight and not give up. Because when my cousin wasn't in the classroom, it was just me. One person in a classroom with thirty-one whites. And that could generate fear. But I don't think I was ever afraid.

I realize the hatred was really ignorance. It was total ignorance. I think that some of the whites really feel bad about the way they treated us and the way they acted toward us. I think they learned that it was not about color. It was about they understand what we were fighting for and why. And I think some are still stuck back in 1968, '67, '66 when I started school.

**Interviewer:** *What's necessary to fix this county? Economically, socially?*

To bury the traditions. Get rid of them. What you was taught. And there's so many people that's stuck in that mindset. Education is—you go to school, and it can take you so far. But learning—there's no end to learning. You have to have an open mind to learn. You need an open mind to learn two and two is four. So you have to have an open mind to learn, you can grow if you want to. To make Benton County a prosperous county, you have to move those people into that mindset that things have to be done a certain way. Your mind has to be opened up, and be willing to accept change.

# Katie Reaves

## 1949–2010

Interviewed September 2003, Ashland, Mississippi, by Aviva Futorian, Roy DeBerry, and John Lyons; and January 2009, Washington, DC, by John Lyons

*Ms. Reaves is the older sister of Rosa Evans. Although she contracted polio when she was a child, resulting in a lifelong dependence on crutches, the affliction didn't detract from her desire to be totally independent. She desegregated Ashland in 1965, when she was in the ninth grade. After her interviews, she became heavily involved in this oral history project, and served as the Hill Country Project's office manager and outreach coordinator. In 2008, a few years before her death, Ms. Reaves traveled to witness the inauguration of Barack Obama. This conversation was edited from a few interviews, both in her home and en route to Washington, DC.*

◆ ◆ ◆

Well, it was my parents' decision to integrate. But I wanted to go. It was something different. I wanted to find out what it was all about. What was different between, you know, black and white. I went to get a better education.

**Interviewer:** *Did your parents give you any advice before you went?*

They told us the truth. They told us that there was going to be some ugly things done to us. But, you know, you just maintain your equanimity. When I first went to Ashland, I really didn't have visions of what to expect. I thought it would be just like it was, going to the all-black school.³ When I was goin' to the black school, you meet people, you sit down, and converse with them.

You made friends. But at Ashland, you really couldn't make friends with them because you don't . . . make friends with those type people.

The first day we got there, it was cold. They acted as though we had some type of contagious disease. When they'd give you something, they wouldn't hand it to you, they'd let it fall to the ground. They didn't want to touch you. They would say to you . . . "You all comin' from *that* school? We don't do this . . ." It's just really hard to describe.

I didn't know it was going to be this hatred that was going on. I don't think they treated me no better than they treated the rest of us. They didn't see me as a person with a disability, they didn't give me no special treatment. They saw me as black. That's what I was to them.

They'd block the sidewalk, you'd have to get off. I got off the sidewalk, walked around, and, you know, minded my own business. I went on and did what I had to do. They would call you "nigger." But, you know, it didn't hurt my feelings. I went on. Calling the names really didn't bother you. Somebody calls you the N-word, you're not supposed to just get up and get angry about that. Maybe it was because you just knew how to move on.

◆  ◆  ◆

They started electing class officers, and we wanted to elect a black person, you know, to the student body. So we all went to the auditorium and there was several of us tryin' to get the principal to acknowledge two blacks. The principal, Mr. Howell, wouldn't acknowledge two blacks, but he would acknowledge two whites. After the meeting was over we, we confronted him in the office about it. So, my sister Carol, along with others, we went to Mr. Howell's office and we wanted to know why he wouldn't acknowledge two blacks. And whether we could put somebody in. Mr. Howell really never gave us an answer. He said to my sister, "Carol, you stay here and the rest of you all go back to your class." I said, "Well, I'm not goin'. I'm not leavin' my sister here by herself." He got angry with us and called the school attorney and the superintendent down on us, Carol and I. He went and got on the phone and called John Farese Sr.[4] And he called the superintendent and they came down here. They wanted to know what the problem was. And we explained to them that Mr. Howell wouldn't acknowledge two blacks but he would acknowledge two whites. If you acknowledge two blacks, then we can elect us a black person. After them comin', we still didn't accomplish anything.

◆  ◆  ◆

High school photo of Katie Reaves.
Courtesy of the Reaves family.

Someone threw a bottle with some type of 'flammatory up in our yard. And a cross was left, yeah. A cross was placed in our yard . . . You knew what it was for. What did Daddy say? We told him, and he said, "Um-mmm." He kind of smiled a little bit. He expected something like that. They did it so they could frighten you. Stop you from doing what you were planning on doing. But we still completed what we was gonna do.

**Interviewer:** *If you had to do it again, would you do it?*

No. It's just a, a bad feeling, you know. Sometimes I think about it. It's just some bitter experiences that I had goin' to Ashland. A lot a humiliation. You were unhappy because you couldn't do the things that you wanted to do there. It's like a strain that's been put on you for life. And you wouldn't want your child to have to go through that. I'm glad that I had the opportunity to integrate the school. I just don't like the way the board of education, the principal, the parents, the students, placed restrictions upon us. Which I know they was doing that to discourage us, but they wanted things their way. It's just a sad feeling to think that somebody would treat you wrong for nothin'. It's just sometimes I wake up and I think I'm still there. I have dreams that I'm still there . . .

◆  ◆  ◆

I can remember that day,[5] where I was. I was in school. And when I arrived home, that evening, there was a sense of quiet in the house. I don't know why, just a quiet day. Then, later on, a bulletin came in and announced Dr. King had been shot at the Lorraine Motel in Memphis and they rushed him to the hospital. A few minutes, they came back and said he expired. Our leader had been gunned down. I had read about him and I had heard my father talking about him. It was a loss, a sadness. It was a hurt that . . . a hurt that you can't hardly describe.

To me, Dr. King saw something in the future. I knew one day there was going to be a black president. I didn't ever think it would be in my lifetime. You can't say that black people elected him, you can't say that white people elected him. You got to say everybody elected this president. Senator Obama, President-elect Obama, is a black man. It's different. On Election Day, I was elated to the point where I jumped up and *whooo*! Hollered real loud . . . I was out there, working, registering. I went into people's home to register people. I met people on the street, and told them to meet me at such and such a place. I carried voter registration forms with me and showed them how to fill it out right. They couldn't leave me until it was done how it was supposed to be done. I carried them to the courthouse, to somebody who was responsible for getting it to the registrar's office. I worked hard.

A lot of people don't understand voting. They say it's not going to help. But this last election here, with President-elect Obama, they saw some results. They can't say it doesn't work. Because it does. Uncle Henry and his wife, my father and my mother were some of the first people to vote in Benton County.[6] And he carried people to the registration office to register to vote. During that time, they had to pass exams to become a registered voter. They would make it very complicated for them to pass it, because they really didn't want black people to vote. The ones that failed, Uncle Henry would carry them back and he would encourage them to keep on tryin' to register. There were people who registered who would be threatened, some of them were killed during that time. I don't think Uncle Henry was frightened about his life, because he never showed he was afraid. He just never showed any fear. I never heard him say anything about stopping. It frightened me then, in a way. But not in a way I couldn't stand up for what I thought was right.

I can't say that civil rights has ended for me or ended as a whole. I'm still doing it. Now, I always carry voter's registration forms with me. I'll start talking with some of the students, "Young lady, are you registered to vote?" "No, ma'am." I'll say, "Come on over and let's get you registered. So you can participate in the elections." People are still doing it. I don't think it's ended. Our journey's not complete. It's not a finished product.

# Ruth Ross

## Born 1948

Interviewed February 2015, Ashland, Mississippi, by Aviva Futorian, Roy DeBerry, and John Lyons

*The daughter of the Reverend John Henry, a.k.a. "Lightnin'" Beard, a prominent and outspoken leader of the movement, Ruth Ross spent her youth as well as her career in the Benton County School System. Being the daughter of a prominent activist meant witnessing her father getting constantly harassed. She vividly recalled instances of intimidation and terror against her family. Rather than deter her father, it inspired him to continue. We spoke with her in the library of Ashland High School.*

◆ ◆ ◆

I was three-and-a-half years old when we moved to Mr. Moody's farm in Ashland. My father was farming at that time, sharecropping. It was like you do the work and the person that owned the farm would get so much of the profit. We would chop the cotton, Dad would get it plowed, and when it come to time to pick it, we gathered it, my brothers and sisters and I. I *could* chop, but I would pick. I would ride on daddy's sack, I would pick and put it in his sack until I got bigger. When I got older, I had my own sack. But we had a comfortable living. I mean, we had plenty of food, we had changin' clothes, which a lot of people didn't have at that time.

The landowners had a daughter. Jamie, she was okay. She couldn't come to our house and play. One time, I asked her if she wanted to come and play, but she couldn't. She could not come here to play. We knew she was white, and she knew she was white.

I remember once I asked my daddy (I was about maybe three or four years old) why we were one color and they were another color. And he gave me the

The Reverend John Henry "Lightnin'" Beard. Courtesy of Frank Cieciorka.

answer, "This is the way God made us." But he always would explain to us that there was a reason behind everything. And as I got older (I was about thirteen then, I think), I asked him, "Why was there so much difference?" We went to the courthouse, and I asked him, "Why was there a black bathroom and why were there a white bathroom? Why is the fountain not the same?" And he told us that we wasn't supposed to drink nor eat with the whites.

**Interviewer:** *Did he say why?*

I don't remember, but as I grew older, I learned. "Wow!" You know? That this is the way they wanted it. That's the only answer I had at that time.

**Interviewer:** *Tell us about your first instance with civil rights.*

I was younger, still at home. We used to go over to, I think it was, Nelma Tipler's place over there. It was a building[7] over in that area. We used to go over there to meetings. My father wanted us to know what was going on. He wanted us to be involved. And he always would tell us—it wasn't a day went by that he did not tell us—"You have to remember you're black. And you'll always be treated different." And on our way back from the meetings, my goodness! We would have to sing. And pray. Because people would just be on daddy, bumping his car. White people were running into the back of his car. Daddy would always say to us, "You hold on, guys. And take care." We were singing. We would sing gospel songs.

◆  ◆  ◆

I remember after we had moved off of Mr. Moody's Farm, there were people come through with masks on, burning crosses in our yard. I was a daddy's child, I was on my dad's knee all the time. And when they would do it, Dad would always tell us not to move. He was a tall man and I was maybe halfway up his body. He told me, "Look at them in the eyes. Don't ever run from them." And that's what I did.

**Interviewer:** *And what happened when you looked them in the eyes?*

They just continued to burn the cross and leave us, like they would normally do. I thought it was horrible that everybody couldn't get along. The only sense I had of that was because we were black. And black wasn't likable. I asked somebody one time, the white lady my mother used to work for (I think I was about sixteen or seventeen) I asked her, "Why don't whites like blacks?" "Because," she said, "White was right and black was wrong." She told me that.

Daddy always said he got involved because he wanted us to have the same rights as the whites have. I remember him telling us that. He would always tell us to do what we were supposed to do. So we would always, if we ever got the opportunity to vote, we could. We could cast our vote any way we like.

I never was afraid for my daddy because my daddy was a firm, strong man that believed in what he believed in. I think the thing that he was let down by most was the people not getting up and going to vote when they had an opportunity to. Because so many people had fought for this opportunity. People had died, you know? People take it for granted now.

It's not the same today. It's better in a sense. I have my children. And I told them what my daddy taught me. That they could be, they could go, they could do whatever they wanted to in life, regardless of white, black, blue, or green. And I instill it in them. I may have instilled it too much. But yeah, it's better. It's a headache in some places, you know, because some people never change. It's better in a sense because most the children now have the opportunity to go to any school they like. And they have it pretty good. They have to work a little, but they have pretty well the opportunity to go someplace and do something with their lives. It's not what it could be, or what it should be. But it's better than it was.

# Peggy Simpson

## Born 1953

Interviewed February 2015, Lamar, Mississippi, by Aviva Futorian, Roy DeBerry, John Lyons

*The sister of Ruth Ross and youngest daughter of "Lightnin'" Beard, Ms. Simpson desegregated the Ashland School in 1966 and was the only one of the Rev. Beard's children to graduate from high school. Like her sister, she recalls nights of harassment by the Klan. She expressed a degree of militancy in the need to respond to those threats.*

◆ ◆ ◆

Daddy was a sharecropper, when you live on other people's land. You live with them and you "share." You pick cotton, and they pay you what they're going to pay you. Actually, you do the work, and they get the pay, and then they pay you. But you live on their land. It felt like it was like slavery. Now, when I got big enough to know anything, they did not treat us like slaves. I said it was kind of like slavery because you lived on their place and you picked the cotton. It just kind of put you in the mind of that, the way the situation was set up.

I can remember when I was about five, six, when I started picking cotton. I guess I knew the difference between white and black, because I understood that I had to totally give the white people respect. I had to—"Mister and Missus," "Yes, sir," and "No, sir," and all that, you know. Couldn't disrespect them no kind of way. Daddy talked about it. I asked him, "How come I have to say, 'Mr. Moody,' and his daughter could say, 'Lightnin''?" That was his nickname, my daddy's nickname. And he explained, you know, because that's just the way it was, because they was white and we was black.

He used to talk about that, that he hoped better would come. He always hoped that better would come for us. That's why when the civil rights got there he jumped on it.

I guess my first memory, I remember meeting workers. And they explained what civil rights was about. It was to help us have the rights that the white people had, and to be treated fair. They were talking about black people getting our rights. And the children getting a fair education and being treated fair, like the white kids, and respect. They were working for all that. I didn't understand very much, because honestly, I really didn't care. Because I knew that meant I was going to have to integrate the school. And I really didn't want to do that. I didn't want to go to school with the white kids. My father made me. Because if it was left up to me, I wouldn't have never went. How did he say it? It was to help the black people. He told me it was a good thing for me. It was to have respect, get a good education, just like them. He felt like I had as much right to have what the white kids had. When he made his ruling, he made his ruling. That was just it. But I didn't see where it was a good thing.

I was in the eighth grade when we integrated. From the first day, I didn't like it because the teachers, they acted as though we was . . . I don't know, how you would put it politely? Like we didn't exist. It was just like we wasn't there. They were talking around us and over our heads, just to the white kids. And they tried to ignore the black children. Because they didn't want to teach us. I didn't want to be there no more than they wanted me to be there, but I didn't have no choice.

◆ ◆ ◆

The Klan was the people that was against civil rights and the blacks getting ahead. The black ones that participated more deeply with civil rights is the ones that they tried to scare. And my father was one of them. We had about three crosses burned in our yard. And we used to have people out at night, out in our yard. Talking and doing stuff around our house. Because, you know, in the summer you have windows up. And you could hear them out talking in the yard, there in the backyard and around. One night, me and my mother were listening out the bathroom window. And we heard them call my father's name. And I think my mother got my father up. They was talking about burning. I don't know, we didn't know, if they was talking about burning the house up or what. But we heard them. And my mother got my father up. And he got his gun, and he went there shooting in the air.

**Interviewer:** *Did you or your mother or anybody else try to stop him?*

No we didn't. Because that's what we wanted him to do, to get rid of them. I really wanted him to shoot *them*, not shoot *at* them.

I don't know if anybody else was having that many problems. But it didn't matter. It wasn't going to stop him from doing what he was doing. But we just went along with it. Because he always would say it didn't matter what they did. It wasn't going to stop him from doing what he wanted to do and was going to do. And really I never sat down and just talked to Daddy about all of this. Because I knew why they was doing it. I didn't have to ask. I knew why. Because Daddy was so into his civil rights, and we was integrating schools. And, like I said, everybody knew him. They was trying to scare him. I did fear for my father, because I feared that maybe when he was out sometimes away from the house, preaching or something. And I was afraid that they might would have killed him while he was out, before we got home.

◆ ◆ ◆

A lot of the white kids, their parents put them in private school. We had a doctor, Dr. Gray. He built a private school.[8] And a lot of the white kids was taken out of there and put into the private school. Those that couldn't afford it had to stay [at the Ashland School]. Over time, I guess I'd say we was there about a year, things got to getting a little bit better. We was being recognized more in the class. And they would talk to us better, the teachers, and was teaching us better. Helping us better. The teachers, I don't guess they were bad. I would say they were more prejudiced than bad. I was kind of, how would you put it? Stubborn. Didn't care. And I guess I got to about the eleventh grade before I really started caring. I started to care so I could hurry up and get out of school. When I first got there, they flunked me. I tried to get Daddy to not let me go. And he wouldn't, so I had to repeat that grade. And see, that wasn't helping any, as I didn't want to go as it was. And then when I seen that he wasn't going to come and back me, then I'm like, "Why you making me do this? And when I need you, you ain't here for me?" I wanted to drop out of school, and my daddy made me stay. I was angry about that because the other ones dropped out. It was six of us Beard children, but I was the only one graduated school.

**Interviewer:** *How did you feel when you graduated?*

It felt good. I was a happy black person. [Laughs.]

I got just as good an education at the black school as I did at the white, because I was more into it, when I was in the black school. I learned more, because I paid more attention. I think the point of going to Ashland School—it was just time for us to be together. I really don't think it was getting a better education in the white school because they taught the same things that the black school taught. I learned as much there as I did at the black school. To me, I think it was that black folks just wanted to show the white folks what we could do. And there wasn't no more "whites here" and "blacks there." We all were going to be together.

It was a good idea. When I got grown and I looked back over the times, I guess that's when I got to realizing what it was for. And it was for a good reason. Because my children didn't have to go through it, and it made it better and easier for my children.

**Interviewer:** *What if your children did have to go through it? Would you have sent them to a white school or let them decide?*

Hmmm . . . I think I would have sent them to the white school. I wouldn't have gave them any choice. To prove a point, that they are just as good as they are, the whites. Because I think that was the point, some of the point, that my daddy was making with me by sending me and integrating the school. He was wanting me to see that point.

I talk to my children about it. The burning crosses, the KKK, integrating. I've discussed all that with them, the history. How I got where I got, and then to live to be a mother. And it's a blessing that I be at where I am in life.

# Anthony and Ernestine Royston, Christine Smith

Born 1954 (Anthony), 1955 (Ernestine), 1954 (Christine)

---

Interviewed November 2014, Potts Camp, Mississippi, by Aviva Futorian, Roy DeBerry, and John Lyons

---

*The Royston Farm area, near Potts Camp in the southwestern part of the county, is peppered with several members of the extended Royston family. Several months after our initial conversation was postponed due to sudden illness, Anthony Royston and his wife, Ernestine, welcomed us into their home. Joining the conversation at the kitchen table was Ernestine's sister, Christine.*

◆ ◆ ◆

**Interviewer:** *What was your first realization that there were white people and black people and they were different or treated differently?*

**Christine:** We had land of our own. But I never understood why we weren't living on that land in the beginning. We lived on the white man's land. We picked cotton and chopped cotton and somehow, I know, we never came out even. I was too young to understand. But Daddy would always say, "We only got so much that we can do. Look like we can never come out even." Alfred Doyle was the owner and he had two sons, Gene and Thomas. His sons were just like family. Gene would come out and sit on the porch and talk. I remember that real good. He used to carry me around on his back. They ate *with* us.

And Mom worked all the time for the Hines, I grew up around Mr. Curtis and Frank. Frank played with a lot of other black guys. And I don't think he treated them any different. I don't think Frank really treated anybody any different.

**Ernestine:** In summers, we would go to the Hines' house. We go into their house, have whatever they had to eat, sit at the table. The way they treated us—it was respect.

**Christine:** So, we were around white people all the time.

**Ernestine:** I think, by that kind of treatment, we were looking for that from others. But we were soon awakened in a different manner. Later on, we learned that it wasn't the way they were.

**Christine:** We moved off the white man's land. My dad somehow got enough money for he and my grandfather to build a house, a little off of that same white man's land. That man came and tried to take the land that my daddy had built the house on. They tried to take the land. I can't remember too much. I just knew that daddy had got a lawyer, and I remember there was a whole lot of stuff going on. And the lawyer that Daddy got helped us keep that land.

**Anthony:** My father and my uncle, they had their own property, but they kind of did like sharecropping.[9] They would go out and help other people. And I could remember years ago—I was small, I guess, maybe five or six. Because we were sharecroppers, we would help white people. We got paid, but it wasn't a fair payment. And it took a while for me to understand what was going on because we shared, we're helping white people and then they wouldn't help us, in some manner or some form. And they would come, I don't know who it was, but they would come and burn crosses in our driveways.

**Interviewer:** *Why?*

**Anthony:** I had no . . . I was young. I can just remember those incidents.

◆  ◆  ◆

**Christine:** When the school[10] was boycotted, we had Freedom School. Earnestine Evans was one of the teachers. And the Freedom School was at the Hardaways Church. You know what? I never heard of Harriet Tubman or Sojourner Truth until we get to Freedom School.

**Ernestine:** There was this café which we went to, it was right on 72. The Cotton Patch Café. And you go to order food, but you couldn't go get it at the front. You have to go to the back. Even the bathrooms, you have to go to the back. And then they had writing on the door: "black" and then "white."

**Christine:** "Colored." It was "colored."

**Ernestine:** Yes. It was "colored" at that time. "Colored" and then "white." There was a sit-in at Cotton Patch Café.

**Christine:** I can't remember who it all was. But I just remembered, I know Fred Richards was one of them. And they carried him to jail.

**Interviewer:** *In the fall of '66, you learned that there was Freedom of Choice and you could go to Ashland School with white kids. Why did you decide to go?*

**Ernestine:** At that time, they had . . . peoples would come to different churches, and they explained to us that we had a choice if we wanted to go. Our parents talked to us, and they insisted that we go. They wanted for us to have a better education.

**Christine:** Because my dad always wanted the best for us, even when it come down to school and church. We never had a choice. We did what he said do. I wanted to go because I wanted something different. I could see the difference in the books. Why would I want to take the hand me down books if I can get some new ones?

**Anthony:** I heard about it from my parents and others in the neighborhood. My mother drove the bus for many years when we all went to Old Salem. It was one bus in this area. And it had quite a few children. And when they would pick us up the bus it would constantly quit on us, on the road. We're going to school, it would quit. That hill over there, there have been times that we actually got stuck going up the hill. There was times that the bus couldn't carry us up the hill because the bus was loaded. We had to get off, walk up the hill, wait till the bus get up and I'm cold, I'm wet. We had to get off that bus and walk to the top of the hill and then mama would stop and pick us up and put us back in the bus.

**Ernestine:** Out here it would be the same thing. Bus would get stuck. Somebody had to come pull us out. We sit out there in that cold until somebody came and pulled the bus out, the bus would quit again and you end up being late for school, and all that.

**Christine:** It would be so packed, we had to stand up. All the seats were gone, just stand up, you don't get no seat.

**Anthony:** No heat. No heat is on . . . they had better buses and they had better books and everything. And so most of my neighbors down here, they kind of insisted that we go to Ashland. My oldest brother was one of the first to go to Ashland. Later on, we came along and they insisted. And we started going up there to Ashland.

**Interviewer:** *Had your parents given you any advice?*

**Anthony:** I mean, what not to say and what not to do. Because, I knew. I should watch out. Kind of stay away from the white girls because you get into more trouble there than you would anywhere else. And they always told us they didn't want us fighting in school, you know, that kind of stuff. As for the name-calling, you had to go report it. But who did you report it to? Because most of the teachers were white.

**Christine:** All of them. All of the teachers was white. And had to call on all the strength in me when I got called "nigger" a minute a day. I kind of like ignored it.

**Ernestine:** I first started in the seventh grade. I know the difference was in the grading system. If you don't keep up with your grades, you end up being cheated. And that first six weeks, I was cheated. The teacher give me an "F." I didn't make that "F." I kept all my papers and everything. It surprised me. I don't know who told me to go, I guess my mother, because somebody told me because the teacher didn't. So, I went to the office. And the principal was Mr. Howell. I'm thinking, at first he probably didn't believe me. I know I had to prove that I actually had made the particular grade. I had kept everything that I needed for to prove what I was supposed to get from my grade. So, they did, they changed. I raised my grade because that was the only class that I had an "F" in. I was an honor student during that time.

**Interviewer:** *What surprised you most about white people or white students who went to school?*

**Anthony:** That they would change. That if you had this discussion with them here, and you get them around other white kids they would change. They would treat you totally different. It was like, I don't know . . . it was like they had something to prove to the other kids and so they treated you different when you're around. You could just see in them. When they got around other white people, they have friends and stuff and they treat you different.

**Ernestine:** Like they didn't know you.

**Interviewer:** *Did you ever feel like you wanted to just forget it and go back to Old Salem?*

**Ernestine:** It goes back to my parents. I think they embedded it in us. They instilled it in us before we went there. If we went, they sent us there. So we got to stick it out.

**Anthony:** My parents wanted us to go to school there and I wanted to graduate. I wanted to get my diploma. And so I just played and stuck it up. There was one lady—Ms. Renick, my English teacher. And she sat me down, talked to me. She told me that I wouldn't graduate unless I do better work. And, I mean, she didn't do it in front of the class. She called me to the side, sat me down. I will never forget, she helped me a whole lot. After graduation, I feel like I accomplished something. I graduated from Ashland High. And it wasn't easy. It wasn't easy because from my first day, I knew that all these people that were walking around didn't like me. I knew that they didn't like me but they had to put up with me. So, I was just in class and trying to get out of school.

**Ernestine:** I think it helped, I actually do. It was available for us to make a choice whether or not to go. I think anybody should go about doing, but nothing would be easy.

**Christine:** There's nothing, nothing easy.

**Ernestine:** I was just thinking. You know what really came to me was after this school was fully integrated? At that time it was just a few of us. By time the school got fully integrated, that's how you found out how the whites really felt about us. After school became fully integrated, we don't have any more white kids at the school. It was just about like what we were when we went to Ashland. And so there was a letdown. That was a hurtful thing. Most of all because, it's like they're scared of us now. We went when *all* of them was there, daily. They don't appreciate us, you know? I know why—it had to start through the parents. And a lot of times, kids don't really understand. Even with me being black, I can still be prejudiced. You have to realize yourself that all of us are human beings. It ain't got nothing to do with this or that, but it take you a while to really learn that. I think until you really learn that for yourself, you still messed up.

**Anthony:** It's what we've been taught, how we've been taught. And I guess how they been taught. That we were inferior to them. I never felt that way, but if you think about it, all the history, us being black and them being white. What they'd done to us or what they did to our parents and how they held them down and how they kept them from a lot of things. And it's hard sometimes even now. I think about it, a lot, because of my skin color.

# The Nelsons

Born 1948 (Joe), 1949 (Shirley), 1953 (Alice), 1958 (Jarius)

Interviewed February 2015, Memphis, Tennessee, by Aviva Futorian, Roy DeBerry, John Lyons, and Stephen Klein

*Alice, Joe, Shirley, and Jarius Nelson were the children of sharecroppers. Their landlord was Billy Carpenter, a white man. Despite the fact their parents were living on and dependent on Carpenter for their livelihood, they became active in the civil rights movement, which resulted in the family getting kicked off the land, rendering them homeless. They talked with us in Shirley's home in Memphis, Tennessee, about the day they were evicted, as well as about sharecropping, desegregating schools, and running into Carpenter later in life.*

◆ ◆ ◆

**Shirley:** People thought we had money. Mama would make our bologna sandwich and cookie, and give us a bath before our meal. She'd have our hair pressed. We didn't have money. We was dirt poor, but she had us looking like we had it going on.

**Alice:** Mama would have a baby; the next two weeks, she was back out in the field. Had that big, long sack on her back. I think that's what killed her, pulling that long sack and then come home with, like, two dollars. All day, two dollars.

**Joe:** Daddy was a hard worker. I've seen my daddy work till he couldn't work no more. Daddy used to work in the fields, all day, and then come in and sleep. And then he had to go down to the Cotton Patch Café and work down there till about two o'clock or three o'clock in morning. And then come home and get him a little sleep, and then ride that tractor all day long. It wasn't never right to me because we never did have anything, you know? Everyone else had bicycles and stuff.

**Shirley:** And I think I always knew it was wrong because . . . you're right here, on the edge, and you're *scraping*. You know something wasn't right. Something ain't right in the world.

**Interviewer:** *Tell us about what sharecropping was about.*

**Joe:** They give you so much land to farm. It was cotton, mostly. When the cotton got big enough to harvest, we went out there and picked the cotton. Whatever we made, like fifteen bales, he[11] got half of that from the crop. And then the other half, he took half of that for himself, too. And then we had to pay for whatever fertilizer or whatever out of the third, I guess. So most time, it was near nothing.

**Alice:** *Zero.* We hardly went to school, picking and chopping cotton for Billy Carpenter all the time. He was a lowdown, dirty dog.

**Shirley:** My dad started to want to be involved in the movement. He was going to this church where you would meet, and we'd talk about civil rights things. Billy didn't like that. Gave him an ultimatum.

**Joe:** "Either the kids go to school[12] or either you gonna have to get off of my land."

**Shirley:** We got off his land. He gave us till five o'clock that evening, till sundown, to get off. So we had to go find some neighbor's big old truck, and we had to go find somewhere to go.

**Jarius:** They was saying that we have to be gone before it got dark. I remember that, as a little boy. We had to be loaded and off the road before it got dark.

**Shirley:** He would have came and shot Daddy—

**Joe:** Or either the Ku Klux Klan would've come to the place.

**Shirley:** Daddy had to find himself and his kids somewhere to live. It was a old house, a raggedy shack, holes in the roof everywhere. And it was sitting up, but nobody was using it. Way back up in the woods. But we weren't unhappy because we was with my daddy and mama. That's all we knew.

**Interviewer:** *How did they explain it to you? Why you had to move?*

**Joe:** Back in them days, you know, parents didn't have to explain too much to they kids, you know? It's the way it was.

**Alice:** And we just did what we were told.

**Interviewer:** *What did your dad do then to make a living?*

**Alice:** I remember Mama saying sometimes he used to walk to Ashland. Went all the way to Ashland, hoping to find some kind of little job to do so he could buy food for the house. And sometimes he would just come back with maybe a sack of flour because he didn't get no work that day, you know—just something to help, you know, to feed us. Mama made a garden and she canned the food.

**Jarius:** And, during the cold season, we would kill a couple of hogs and that would take us through the winter up until the summer.

**Interviewer:** *How long did you stay there?*

**Jarius:** A long time. Ten or eleven years.

**Shirley:** I admire them, how they could take *nothing*, and make something out of it. To fill a belly, you know? And it wasn't about Mama. It was about her children. She let her children eat first because she wanted to make sure that they were full. They worked hard, Mama and Daddy, and that's where I learned. If I don't have nothing else in this world, I am a strong black woman. I can take care of myself.

**Interviewer:** *Did your parents stay active in the movement?*

**Alice:** I remember going to the meetings.

**Joe:** Samuel's Chapel, Macedonia, Mount Zion. They used to talk about registering to vote. Yes, voting.

**Shirley:** And we would sing the songs. "Don't Let Nobody Turn You Around."

**Joe:** I was young. It didn't mean nothing to me. I wasn't scared. We're just going to a freedom meeting, you know? But the older peoples, they knowed what it was all about. They was scared. The churches was getting blowed up. You had to be careful going down that road, because you'd be scared the Klan is gonna drop by and shoot you or run you off the road.

◆ ◆ ◆

**Shirley:** They didn't tell me, "You have to go to integrate the schools." It was my choice. It was the people in the church where we went for the those freedom meetings, they was recruiting kids to go. And I said I wanted to go. I thought the whites would accept us a little better. I should've known better than that. I only did one year over there because I left, went back to Old Salem. I didn't like it. The teachers didn't treat you right. You know, you could tell that it was a difference. They would kind of say little remarks to you, like we were stupid. And the kids, when you walk down the hall and you'd feel something, they'd throw water on you or spit on you or something. Call you names behind your back.

**Jarius:** When I first went to Ashland, it was grammar school. Second grade. I didn't have a choice. I didn't want to go there, to tell the truth. And we had to stay with Alice when we first went there. And she kept us under her up there. Alice took care of a lot of the younger children. We was scared, you know? We didn't know what was going on. I had never went to school with a bunch of white folk. We just went to have a better life and get better teaching. But to me, I don't see how it was better teaching when we're being mistreated. We couldn't ride on the front seat, but we had to ride at the back of the bus. When we'd got off the bus, they would holler at the bus driver, "Why you let these 'N's' ride the bus with us?"

**Alice:** They just didn't like us, and they thought we was nothing. But I didn't let them talk crazy to me, not even the principal. He tried to make me and my sister Dean go to the back of the bus. I was in about the ninth grade, something like that. We was tired of sitting at the back of the bus. We was sitting in front, maybe about the third seat. And the bus driver said, "Get to the back of the bus." I said, "I'm not going nowhere." And he sent somebody in there to get the principal, that big old Mr. Robinson. He come out there with the big strap. "Get to the back of the bus." My sister, she was crying. I told her, "If you move, I'm gonna kill you." We didn't move. I didn't say a word to him. He kept on hollering. He said, "Move to the back of the bus. Move to the back of the bus!" I ain't say a word. I thought he was gonna hit me. But he said, "Well, this gonna be your seats from now on. You sit in these seats." And he went on about his business.

**Interviewer:** *Where'd you get the courage?*

**Alice:** From my daddy. I just saw how strong he was, that he just didn't let nothing get to him. My mama was strong, too.

**Interviewer:** *Did you ever run into Billy Carpenter? Later in life?*

**Jarius:** I did. I was probably nineteen or twenty at the time. We used to go to a church, and I used to see him up by the Cotton Patch Café up there. And he would come up there and he was beginning to have Alzheimer's. He couldn't remember where he was supposed to go. He couldn't remember where he lived. One time he asked me, "I can't remember nothing on my own. Do you know where I live?"

He pulled out a bunch of hundred-dollar bills, and he says, "I'll pay you to tell me where it's at." I said, "You ain't got to pay me. You live right there" [points]. He got in his truck and went straight up the hill, and said, "Thank you, son. Thank you."

When I would tell folks about that night, they'd say, "I would've took his money." Naw, I *couldn't*. I couldn't take his money. I just wouldn't want the man to pay. I'm a Christian, and I didn't, you know, want to do him like that. With Alzheimer's. I knowed him. You can't mistreat others.

**Interviewer:** *If you had a choice to go to integrate school again, would you do it?*

**Alice:** To make it better for somebody else coming along, I would.

**Shirley:** Sure. I'd go, and I'd know how to work that thing. Because I would know how to talk to them now. And I would know how to approach them. I would probably say, "Why you don't like me? What have I done to you?" And I'd just wait on the answer, and they wouldn't have an answer. That's what I would say if I could. But I wouldn't be mean or nothing, and want to hurt nobody. I never did.

**Jarius:** Okay. I would stay in the black school. But see, even when we went to the white school, all the white folk left the school. And it ended up being back to a black school.

**Interviewer:** *Was school integration a waste of time?*

**Jarius:** I don't think it was. You know, a lot of folks lost their life, trying to make it better for us, you know. Even a lot of white folks lost their life, trying to stand up for black folks.

**Alice:** Well, I tried, you know. I would get along with anybody. It seemed like, you know, when you try to be nice, there's always gonna be . . . some that don't like you. In my perspective, they didn't like black folks, for some reason. "What did we do? I didn't do nothing to you. You had everything. I didn't have nothing. Why you hating me?" I should hate you, but I don't. I don't see why they hated us.

Citizens Club Meeting, March 16, 1965.
Courtesy of Frank Cieciorka.

Civil rights meeting, 1965. Courtesy of Frank Cieciorka.

Civil rights meeting,
1965. Courtesy of
Frank Cieciorka.

Mount Zion Church.
Courtesy of Frank
Cieciorka.

Samuel's Chapel meeting.
Courtesy of Frank Cieciorka.

Civil rights meeting,
summer 1965. Courtesy
of Frank Cieciorka.

Bobbie Steward, Naomi Reaves at a civil rights meeting, 1965. Courtesy of Frank Cieciorka.

Civil Rights meeting at Mount Zion. Courtesy of Aviva Futorian.

# Chapter 4

# WHITE REACTIONS

*The tumultuous events of the 1960s had a profound effect on everyone involved: African Americans who were leading the movement, observers who were watching from a distance, and white people who found themselves in the middle of a rapidly changing world. "To keep a man in a ditch, you have to be there with him" was something Aaron Henry, the cousin of Ginevera Reaves and the leader of the state NAACP, would often say. One of the ideals of the civil rights movement was that equality would make everyone more free, regardless of race. The problem was fear, and the mythology (the Lost Cause) of some white people that, for others to gain more rights, they themselves would have to give up some. Whites, especially poor whites, frequently responded to this change in the status quo with fear, leading to hate and violence.*

# Carlton McKenzie

## Born 1958

---

Interviewed October 2005, Ashland, Mississippi, by Aviva Futorian, John Lyons, and Stephen Klein

---

*Mr. McKenzie was a white first-grader at Ashland when desegregation began. His family moved away to the Gulf Coast of Mississippi when he was in fourth grade and returned for his senior year of high school. He attended Ashland High School, which by that point had become mostly black. At the time of our interview, he was a part-time mechanic, and he welcomed us into his garage. Observing us, but not taking part in the conversation, was his nineteen-year-old daughter, Courtney.*

◆ ◆ ◆

I was brought up in Benton County. Our family has always been pretty much based out of Benton County. My father had a little farm. And we've always worked around or been with white and black people. We had a lady that cleaned the house, she practically raised us. I was brought up to believe that everybody is equal. I've always had black friends, and I still have black friends to this day that I graduated with, that I consider good friends of mine.

**Interviewer:** *Did your parents or any adult ever talk to you about the difference between black and white people?*

Well, no, as far as a difference. We just, we all knew. My belief is that you stick with your race. I mean, you know, not saying one's better than the other but just saying that that's what . . . that is my opinion. You stick with your race.

There was two black children that I remember. Leroy Richard and Gertrude Richard. They were the first two I remember going to school with me. I remember distinctly how smart Leroy and Gertrude both are. They were very, very intelligent people. You know, I was a child, I didn't think much about it. I watched it on TV and the big cities where the rioting started and all. You know, it never was . . . I was young, I didn't think very much of it.

I was in Benton County school till fourth grade. My two uncles opened a grocery store similar to 7-Eleven. It's called Junior Food Mart. My father went down there to help in the store. And that's when we moved and I went to Pascagoula, Mississippi. That's where first time I really recognized the racial trouble. It was just more or less blacks against whites. Just a big city school and you know, it just had more trouble there. I personally didn't have any racial problems. I went to school with some people that *did* have racial problems. They did not get along with the blacks or whatever they just didn't . . . they did not agree. It was just a very bad situation a lot of times.

We sold our store and we moved back to our home. My father was in poor health. In 1974, I believe it was. We moved between eleventh and twelfth grade that summer. And I graduated at Ashland High School. If I'm not mistaken about this . . . in my high school graduating class, I believe there was twenty-eight boys and three or four were white, and the rest were black.[1] It could get uncomfortable. Given my experience in Pascagoula, I didn't know what to think. I did not know what to expect. But I walked in with a good attitude and it paid off. I got to be friends with a lot of people there. Graduated from high school, married a girl from Benton County, Janice Berg, with two children. I drove a truck for twenty-two years. I've been on disability because of my heart, my lungs, all of it combined. I work when I have to. I have to do what I have to do to make a living yes. I buy and sell cars to try and make extra money. I have two children. Courtney and Carlton McKenzie, twenty-one and nineteen.

**Interviewer:** *Are you aware of what's happened in the schools in Benton County? That the Ashland School is over 90 percent black and Hickory Flat is over 90 percent white.*

Am I aware of it? Yes, I am. And the reason for this is the intertwining of the couples. That's why they do it. Black and white. Black and whites marrying each other, I do not believe in that. You just don't do that. I mean it's not, I try not to say anything bad about the black or whatever color . . . I don't think it's proper.

**Interviewer:** *What does that have to do with—*

Schools? It keeps the kids apart. We in the workforce will always have to interact. But as a child I do not believe that you need to be . . . I was raised up around black kids. And they wouldn't date white people. And I'm not gonna date black people. And I got black friends. They wouldn't date a white girl because it's . . . the children would never be accepted. I'm not asking other people to do the same as I am. All I do is I do it my way. But when you have that much ya know . . . how often does a parent actually get to see his child? I was a truck driver twenty-two years. I was home only on weekends, and I got to spend very few hours a week with my children. Okay? How am I gonna raise in my daughters my belief in just a few hours a day? But if you're going to school every day five days a week, people teaching you that it is okay.

**Interviewer:** *If your son came home one day and said, "I know how you feel but I've fallen in love with a black girl and I'd like you to meet her . . ."*

The first thing he needs to do is get all his stuff and get his ass out of my house. That's something I believe in. If my daughter was to . . . you can ask my daughter right now what I'd do to her. The only thing I could tell her is, "You've got to go." As far as I'm concerned, I never want to see you again. And never will. It's just . . . it's just my way. Right or wrong. And I'm not saying anything against the black people. I have some great black friends. And that's where I would prefer my kids to draw the line. You can be friends. You can play ball together. But when it comes to personal relationships that's where you draw the line. I do not, as long as I got a breath in me, I don't believe its gonna happen.

I see more of a problem now with the white people being discriminated against as I do the black. Black people right now are more racial than the white people. They have more problems. Everybody always wants to blame the white man for this, the white man for that. We all have equal opportunities nowadays. Almost. Because if you go try to get a small business loan with the government helping now, if you're not black, a woman . . . a black and a woman can get a loan, a small business loan quicker than anybody right now. Being supposedly the minority. I think it's bullshit. I think that we all be, it ought to be all based upon the person, the individual. Not what color you are. Not what, if you're male or female. On what you have done in your past. And what you, you know, that's what I believe it ought to be based on.

# Wyatt Thomas

## 1919–2011

Interviewed January 2004, Michigan City, Mississippi, by Aviva Futorian, and John Lyons

*A Benton County native, Mr. Thomas was a white landowner who had sharecropping families on his farm. The families could never get ahead financially because the system Mr. Thomas and other landowners utilized kept them in perpetual debt and servitude. He was deeply suspicious and critical of the civil rights movement. We interviewed Mr. Thomas at the house on his farm.*

◆ ◆ ◆

My granddaddy's people came down here from North or South Carolina, after the Civil War. They settled in this area and all of them I knew of were farmers. They bought this land (I don't know who they bought it from), but they bought way back in the early 1900s. They had in the neighborhood of three thousand acres.

School? We had the old one-teacher school. It was right down here in Spring Hill behind my house where I lived. They had the same thing, what you call Old Salem—the colored school. What I am trying to say is, they had the same facilities so forth as the whites did up there. I think they had the same books and everything. We just kind of . . . we go here and they go there. And that's about the extent of it.

**Interviewer:** *And when you finished school, what did you do?*

Started farming. We had mostly cotton, and quite a few cows. I took up this place when my daddy died. He had fourteen families of sharecroppers. The person that owns the land and all paid for everything. And the sharecropper

Wyatt Thomas in his home after our conversation. Courtesy of
John Lyons.

had a certain area, a certain crop in that area. He gets half of the return, and
the landowner would get half. They wouldn't get paid anything until after the
harvest. We furnished everything, we would advance them money to buy them
clothes, and that would come out of half of their crops at the end fall.

**Interviewer:** *And how profitable was it for you?*

It broke me. We had three or four bad crop years. One time, it frost so early and
it killed all of the crops before it procured [matured], you see? And another
year I had a boy who couldn't read or write, and instead of killing weeds he
put out poison to kill the grass and he killed the dang cotton. Put me down
so bad that I had to sell some land to get out of debt. It was in about 1942 to
'43, up in that area.

**Interviewer:** *So what did you do next?*

I was a county supervisor sixteen years, second district. The supervisors kept
the roads, that was about the extent of it. And then I went back on this old
farming [chuckling].

**Interviewer:** *People say that there was a lot of racial violence in Mississippi,
early on in the century.*

You know why they were lynching them? Because they had killed several white peoples.

The worst one that I know about, three white men—two of them died and one was left. They went up and robbed him and killed him, you see. The niggers left and that's when the lynching come on. Everybody was so upset at the ones who did it—they killed a man and he was just a little deputy. He went to these people and when he went up to the house, they were down there selling corn whiskey I think. Anyhow, they were breaking the law. He went up to arrest them and they opened the door and shot him. White fellow, and that caused a public disturbance, I guess.[2]

Being raised with them, I know the habits of them and they don't have any morals, really. A lot of older ones go to church. I don't want to say they don't have the same feelings towards the neighbors or something, but they want all they can get out of you, money-wise, most of them. They want something for nothing, is my idea.

**Interviewer:** *If they would have kept separate facilities and kept segregation, do you think that that would have worked?*

It felt like it could. I'm not saying that . . . I know they all need help and all, but it looked like they were taxing me to help them. That is, they weren't paying any part of their share. To me, that's just my opinion.

**Interviewer:** *You didn't think the civil rights movement was on the right path?*

I don't think so. It looks like they could have gone at it in a different . . . just because they were black they didn't have to work. We worked for what we got. Don't you think they should have to work for what they get?

# Mike Carroll

## Born 1957

Interviewed March 2010, Ashland, Mississippi, by Aviva Futorian and John Lyons

*An entrepreneur with boundless energy, Mr. Carroll sat down with us in his antique shop in Ashland. His job as a flight attendant takes him frequently around the world; the artifacts of these trips are found throughout the store. He and his partner Tim (who, having wed in 2015, are among the only openly gay couples in Benton County) own a successful restaurant in New Albany. He has become active in not only local business but politics as well. After two unsuccessful runs for mayor of Ashland against his brother, to whom he lost by tens of votes, he served on the Ashland Town Council. He was attending Ashland in fifth grade when desegregation began, and stayed for a few years after. Eventually he was one of the many white students who wound up attending Gray Academy, a private school created in the mid-1960s as a haven for white students to avoid integration.*

◆ ◆ ◆

My great-grandmother was Native American. She was from this area, the north Mississippi area. My great-grandfather was a civil war officer. My great-grandparents are still buried right here, near town. My father's buried right here in the Ashland cemetery. We have quite a history from this area.

Benton County came to be in 1870 or 1871. The primary city here was Salem. Salem existed about three to four miles from the center of Ashland. It was a pretty thriving community, and even though a lot of people will tell you it's not true, Salem was a slave trade center for this area. It was also a home for Nathan Bedford Forrest.[3]

With the northern forces coming through, they bombarded Salem just about every opportunity that they had. I believe for those two reasons. One, it was a slave trade center, and they were also looking for Nathan Bedford Forrest. At the end of the war, they were pretty much living like Katrina victims out in that area. And beginning with 1870, they began to bring about a town, Ashland.

And, the property for the town of Ashland to be built on, was given by a Mr. McDonald. He gave the property for Ashland to be built on. And some land that he gave was for the school to be founded on. And in the town's commitment to Mr. McDonald, for the school property, it was stipulated there was supposed to never be a black child to attend school there.

◆ ◆ ◆

A pretty confounding moment in my life, I think I was five years old: Our next-door neighbor was a JP, or justice of the peace. Mr. Gross. And he happened to be teaching a black minister whose name was Lightnin'[4] how to read. And someone, I assume, now being as young as I was, wasn't happy with the fact that he was teaching him how to read. And I looked out the bathroom window to see a cross burning in his yard.

For five years old, it was, pretty earth-shaking. So I asked my parents what was going on. And they, as best they could, tried to teach a five-year old, you know, what's going on in the world. They said, "Well, they're burning that cross in the neighbor's yard probably because he's teaching Lightnin' how to read." My parents explained to me that there are some people who believe that others should not be quite as educated. "Others," is how they put it. My dad had grown up in Tubby Bottom. And, in that area, he had blacks help him farm the land that they had almost lost many years earlier. If it hadn't been for his black friends, they probably would have. My dad was a very even-keeled fella. We were always taught everyone was equal. Regardless of skin color, regardless of background. And I'm sure growing up next door to Mr. Gross had an impact, also.

I was really happy when Murray Reaves[5] got to come to school with me. Because we had been friends before. My parents, my dad especially, and Walter Reaves, were friends. My first experience with school integration was when Freedom of Choice[6] came. And, specifically when Murray came to Ashland School. I believe I was in the fifth grade when that took place, would've been around 1967. For a lot of people it was very traumatic. It was, "You know, we've got black kids"—of course, they didn't use the words "black kids" at the time—"coming to *school* with us." And some people thought that it was absolutely abhorrent. School integration, I think, brought in a lot of the white anger. School integration stirred it up. Those years preceding it, I think they were probably some of the most hateful years around here.

Before that, you had separate schools. But you had, I think, a little more respect between those of the different races, especially for us as kids. Some of us thought, "Well, what's the big deal? We've known these kids." And that may've been the difference. Some of us knew these kids, closer than others did. We knew them as people, instead of a black child. So I think that made a big difference for a lot of us.

There were many times the black kids were treated very cruelly. They were heckled. If they were walking the sidewalk, they would be tripped. Lot of kids wouldn't get on a basketball court with them in the beginning. You know, the white kids, immediately upon integration, a lot of them would just choose not to participate in whatever the black kids were participating in. And then some of us went on with life. I was called a nigger lover many, many times. And, it hit me in the face. If I were totally honest, yeah, it, it bothered me as a kid, because . . . you're already carrying a crutch around because you have friendships with these kids. And then to, be degraded, I guess is the best way to put it. I wasn't the only one who was called a nigger lover, back in those days. I definitely caught a blunt force with it pretty often.

Murray and I, we continued to be friends. We continued to see each there. Needless to say, it was nothing like it had been in the past. You know, there was no way possible. All of a sudden, you know, you have those people who are telling you that all of this was wrong. "They've torn our school down, they've taken our school away from us." It wasn't seen in any way whatsoever in a positive light by most people at that time. Sonny (Henry Reaves Jr.) stood out. It was, of course, known that Sonny was Henry Reaves's son, and that Henry Reaves was very prominent in bringing about the integration process that was taking place here. Sonny was the illusion of one of the big problems with the integration process. Maybe they saw him as being more boisterous about how he felt about what was coming about then. Sonny was definitely treated differently. I saw him tripped on the sidewalk. I heard of stories of kids who would jump Sonny. I did see him heckled. I did see him, you know, kind of chastised for being different. For being black. I think he had to absorb a whole lot more of the hate and bigotry.

I believe it was early 1970 when what came down to being called "forced integration"[7] took place here. And for the whole county, the education system here came to a screeching halt. Everything stopped. When this court order came down, no one [whites] went to school. The schools just seemed to have been abandoned. And everyone was trying to figure out what to do with their kids for school. If I remember, it seemed much longer, but I believe the schools were closed for about three weeks. And, my parents, were like the last holdouts for the white kids around here. Because, they weren't sure what to do with me.

Once they saw that almost all of my teachers left and were teaching at Gray Academy, my folks finally got me in school at Gray Academy. I was probably one of, if not the last one, of the white kids in the area to go.

Gray Academy was a private school that was begun by Dr. William Gray, who was the town's doctor. And he had begun it in about 1963, '64. Somewhere right in that area. I do think it was begun as a result of the apprehension of school integration. I believe that's why a lot of the private schools in north Mississippi began.

**Interviewer:** *There were no black kids there?*

None. At the time that this all took place, it was really strange. All of a sudden, the whole education system here was flipped on its head. My parents' thoughts were getting an education for me, the best education they could. The public-school system did fall apart. There were issues, and a lot of problems. Not brought on by black, not brought on by white, but just because of what had taken place. I think the education system here, in the public school, was lacking. You had such a transference of teachers. I mean, the influences, the people we had working with us in the public school, were now in the private school.

◆  ◆  ◆

I remember that blacks were intimidated into voting as the man, I guess you would say, would want them to vote. Or, stay home from voting, not vote at all. I kind of come from a pretty politically minded family. My dad ran several times for sheriff here, unsuccessfully. I don't know why I kind of got the political mind myself, even as a child. My oldest brother was part of the band who went out and helped sign blacks up to vote here. His name was Ronnie Carroll. And he always was, up until his death, very proud of that fact.

**Interviewer:** *You left Benton County, pretty soon after you graduated.*

Honestly, there was so little here to stay for. I mean, it's just worsened over the years. If you were going to succeed, if you were going to find a viable job, and if you were going to grow, you weren't going to be able to do it in Ashland or in Benton County, Mississippi. So you knew you were going to have to go somewhere else to do that. And I had started to work for the Ford dealership in Holly Springs, and then went onto the Ford dealership in Olive Branch. Then I went on to work for a tune up and oil change chain. I taught customer service for them. Then another company called Cookies Incorporated, which was kind of a Mrs. Fields-type chain of cookie stores. I bought and leased their property and did all their customer service training for them. I left that in 1985 to take a break and become a flight attendant for a couple of years. And now that's been going on twenty-five years. During that time, about sixteen, seventeen years ago, I started up this import business.

When I left here, in 1979, I never thought I would return to Ashland, Mississippi. But an old house that I'd always wanted came on the market that had been in the family since it was built. My mom, even though she would definitely not term herself as elderly, is getting up in the years.

◆ ◆ ◆

I really accepted the fact that I was gay in 1981. I had been married, divorced, and with my old high school girlfriend. And when I finally came to terms with it, as far as knowing, it's always there, but coming to the point of accepting it, which for me was 1981. Sometimes it's pure hell. Sometimes it's the very same type of discrimination that you have witnessed . . . an example would be running for office in this town. I ran for mayor of Ashland twice. Both times, the war drums came out over the gay issue. Signs stuck in the yards of supporters. "How can you call yourself a Christian?" "Repent now." "Ashland does not deserve a gay mayor." That was one nailed to a tree.

**Interviewer:** *You've spent a lot of time away, and then come back. Has Benton County changed?*

I would like to think its improved. But, quite honestly, I think racially, people are accepting other people a little more easily. I think they're accepting opposite races. But I think to be able to really flourish, that we're going to have to do more than just accept. And I don't think we are going past that. I, actually, have seen what I think is Ashland and Benton County, rolled backwards. It's kind of gone backwards. Lot of people will blame that on the integration, on the integration that whole place is drying up. But, in reality, I think it's drying up as a result of people who are not going to accept progress, or integration, of any type here. It still holds us back.

# Linda Davis

## Born 1950

Interviewed September 2013, Snow Lake Shores, Mississippi, by Aviva Futorian, and John Lyons

*Ms. Davis is a Benton County rarity for two reasons. She was born in Montgomery County, Maryland, and was married to a black man, with whom she had two biracial children. Both of those children attended Ashland well after integration began, when it had become mostly black. Originally a teacher, she left school to work at an engineering firm. A desire to be closer to her husband's family brought them to the area of Snow Lake Shores in Benton County, where she returned to teaching part-time. She welcomed us to her home and we had the following conversation in her living room.*

◆ ◆ ◆

December of 1990, we moved to Snow Lake Shores. I am not sure who developed it, but I think it was in the 1950s and it was a resort-type community, very segregated. I'd say probably about three hundred families.[8] When I first got here, I had to laugh at myself because I had worked in Mississippi before when I was with the engineering firm. I was sent to the Vicksburg-Port Gibson area. There was a nuclear power plant and I was down there for almost a year. And at that time, the local people at the power plant wanted to hire me and I said, "No, I am not interested in living in Mississippi." I would never live in Mississippi because of the race relations at that time, around 1982. I just could not cope with the whole Mississippi situation. So then when I ended up back here, I just laughed at myself because I said, "Never." And here I was buying a house in Mississippi. I think I realized after I started teaching in Mississippi that there was a lot that I could provide to students. Students who had never thought outside of Mississippi, who had never been any place and did not know a northern person or a person with a different perspective. It was a good move for me. I felt so much more comfortable in this area than I did where we were living in Maryland. It had gotten so people-packed. I mean, around the Washington, DC, area it was just people everywhere, and this area just gave me a sense of being able to breathe and make friendships and just . . . deal better.

My children are biracial. One of the things I have been upset throughout the whole time I lived here is the fact that the blacks and whites do not mix. I have seen it more in the last ten years, people being more comfortable. But it is still is not spilling over into the churches. It's still a very separate life on Sundays.

**Interviewer:** *Were there any problems with your children?*

With most people, no. Most of the residents, I would say no. We did have some problems with neighbors of my parents who called with threats and such to begin with, but we stayed and they moved.

To my first husband, I consistently said, "No, I am not interested," because it would make my life complicated. But I think as we got closer, he taught me a lot, even though we ended up divorcing. He taught me it's not my problem, it's their problem. So if we ran into problems with other people, he would just say, "Well, that's your problem. If you don't want to be around us or look at our family then move away, get out of the situation." So I think that kind of set me up for being successful. When you looked at our family, there's four different colors: my daughter is very light, my son is darker, my ex was dark. We had a lady come up once and say, "Which one of these kids are yours?" "Well, they *both* are." "But they are not the same color!" So we just said, "None of us are the same color." She said, "I don't understand." I think to deal with it, part of what I feel like we were placed here for a reason. I feel that God put us there because they needed a change. The world is not always like what you think it is.

My children have more diverse friends now as adults than they did when they were growing up. In the school. A large percentage of their classmates were black and so they were pretty much around black children.

I think my own children did not encounter a whole lot of problems because they started through the system very young. My daughter went through Head Start for a couple of years. My son was there. They both went clear through the system. I think that kind of cushioned them against any kind of problems. They were just accepted as some of the children that were always there. Going through the Ashland School System, my children expressed good and bad. They are like night and day. My son is a very social, outgoing young man who loves everybody and will talk to anybody. And my daughter is much more studious and dramatic about everything. So my son thought it was just great because he had a very close-knit group of friends. He knew all the teachers, he knew all the community. At fifteen, he started working at the local grocery store, so he knew everybody, and it was fine to him. He felt like he got a good education. My daughter, at times, expressed that she wished she was in a large system because she wanted more opportunities. She loves science, and the science lab was not up to what she thought it should be, so she whined and cried about that kind of thing. But still she has very close friends from the area now. So I think that was their complaint—that sometimes it was too small that they felt like they didn't get as much opportunity as they wished.

My husband and I both felt like our kids were given advantages by being biracial, and that's what we tried to instill in them. That they have the best of two worlds. That's why we said, "You may be looked at differently by some people, but you have some of everybody in you." So we worked that advantage, plus we were both college educated. I think from an early age, we just made sure our kids had plenty of books and plenty of experiences to kind of help them, guide them.

Since I have been in Benton County, I think the attitudes have changed for the good. Kids are more aware of the world as a whole through technology, through computers, cell phones that they have. I think the younger generation coming up is seeing that the whole world is not like Mississippi. A lot of the younger people are understanding the need for change. Some of the older ones are still very set in their ways, but I am seeing more change in youngsters coming up. Hopefully that will be our saving grace.

# Chapter 5

# OBSERVERS

*Many black people in Benton County were not active in the movement. Fear was a predominant factor. While the onslaught of the civil rights movement was clearly an exciting turn for some of the more active residents, other black Benton Countians were less eager to see the status quo shaken up with uncertain results. The following conversations are with a variety of black residents who observed the movement but never became actively involved.*

# Eldora Johnson

## 1902–2003

Interviewed December 1995, Lamar, Mississippi, by Aviva Futorian

*A retired cafeteria worker in the Benton County School System with a poetic flair for language, Ms. Johnson was ninety-three years old at the time of this conversation. Her grandmother was an enslaved person, and she was born on the Hardaway Plantation in Benton County at the turn of the twentieth century. Her razor-sharp power of recollection produced many memories, most of them painful. Her daughter and son-in-law, Thelma and Loyal Thompson, were two of the leaders of the civil rights movement in Benton County, something of which she was enormously proud. A sense of pride and purpose was abundant in the discussion of her life, with one exception: her unwillingness to get involved in the movement, despite her children's activism. "To tell the truth," she says almost apologetically, "I was just scared."*

◆　◆　◆

I was going to summer school.[1] This was the summer of '34 and I was rooming there; it was too inconvenient for me to go from home up there every day. And they was having school at the white folks' gym;[2] they didn't let us have school in the school house. We was in the gym sitting on bleachers. I had come home on the weekend, my husband came and brought me home. And that Sunday night he's carrying me back. We's going on that night, it was so many cars passed and passed, and my husband say, "It's something going on."

That Monday morning, just as we drove and stopped at the stop light, here comes Ms. Clara Meadow. And she fell upon the car and went to crying. We wanted to know what was the matter. She says, "They done lynched the Houey boy and the Jones boy last night. They lynched them down by Meridian Road." It was a big old oak tree down from the Hardaway Pond, and that's where they hung those boys. They made them get up on the truck, and they was hung, and they drove the truck out from under them and brought them up to the jail and pitched them down on the ground.

It was two brothers had a little old store, and they claim somebody broke in this store, and they put it on those colored boys. It was a Houey and a Jones. So these boys, they arrested 'em and put 'em in jail. And they wasn't in jail long before they was lynched. So we went on to school that day; Sadie Avant and I, we came back that evening, we decided to go up to the jail. The other colored women wouldn't go. We walked up there . . . and they had put 'em up on some kind of scaffold. And one of the boys was real light and the other one was dark. And that light one, you could see where that knot on that rope had scrubbed his skin back under his ear. And they had something spread over them, but the face wasn't covered. Flies was swarming all over. They couldn't get no Negroes hardly to dig the graves. They paid one old man to dig the grave to bury these boys. The Negroes was just naturally scared. It was just dangerous for Negro men to be around white folks.

◆ ◆ ◆

I was the first Negro that integrated the cafeteria employees at Ashland School, where it been all-white. They transferred me in the summer of '59. I worked eleven years at Old Salem, then when they integrated, they chose me. Maude Hensley was the supervisor over the Old Salem lunchroom. She came in and talked with me and asked me, "Will you accept the job at Ashland?" I said, "I rather stay where I am at." I said I never have worked around white people and I figured I be the only black up there and they'll try to put all the hardest work on me. She said it wouldn't be like that. I said, "Well, I'll give it a try. If I don't like it, I said, 'Thank God I got a home to go to because our land was paid for.'"

So a few days before school opened they sent me word to come so we could freshen up the kitchen. When I got there Maude said, "Eldora, say I heard you didn't want to come up here." I said I didn't. She said, "Why?" I said, "Because I am black and I's gone be the only one up here. I never worked around white people. And I figured you all would try to put the hardest work off on me." And she said, "We accepting you as one of us," and she and Mrs. Ford was just as nice to me as if I had been as white as they was.

The children was nice to me, and they knew my cooking. I had to fix all the main dishes after I got to Ashland. But at Old Salem, I helped fix the cobbler pies and rolls and everything. And they could tell when I made my pies, I rolled my dough real thin and crisscrossed my crust on the top . . .

**Interviewer:** *Do you remember when you first heard that there was going to be freedom workers coming into Mississippi?*

One came to my house one Sunday. Had some kind of paper she wanted me to sign. And I told her I wouldn't sign it. I said because you going back where you stay, and I got to live down here 'mongst these white folks. So she didn't try to insist on me. I tell you who really stuck with me. Johnny B. Daugherty, we called him Sugarman. And he'd go off to different meetings and he would bring more information back. He would just tell us 'bout different things going on at the meetings, and didn't too many folks talk with me because I wasn't, you know, going to these meetings. And reason, my husband was sick, it's true. But I could have got a way to go with Nelma or Nelma's mother, but I am a truthful person, I tell the truth: I was afraid.

I was afraid some of the white people, the Ku Klux Klans, may set our house afire or do something . . . I wasn't afraid of the peoples that was trying to help us. I was afraid of the white folks *here.*

One night the Ku Klux Klan came through [autumn 1965]. It looked like a funeral processional. They would start slow—just a line of trucks and cars honking their horns. I got so nervous. And my husband say, "Woman, you come on back to bed. As long as they stay out there in that road, it's all right." He say, "But I know one thing. If they come up in here, they may get me. But I get some of 'em before I go." [Laughter]. He said, "Some of these Negro people running round here, they gon' be swung up to a tree or something." He was scared just like I was. The hurting part about it is the ones that took the risk to make things better.

It was somewhere in the sixties, my daughter and her husband left my house and I heard a car come by driving so fast. They had a cross afire up there at this little office[3] down the road, and my son-in-law Loyal Thompson and Jake Nunnally put that cross out. Jake Nunnally and Loyal Thompson were 'bout the two bravest black men here.

It was so much . . . so much was going on. And the white people, it look like they's talking rougher to the Negroes than they had been. Now my own color, some of 'em got pretty rough with me because I wasn't coming to meetings. They's calling me a Aunt Tom.

My husband was disabled to work for ten years. I knew I had to make a living. Let me tell you what I working for when I was first hired in the lunchroom [at Old Salem]. Annie Mae Webber was the manager; they say I would be the assistant manager. We had to do everything from muscle-beating the bread like at home. Sometime we had to cut those gallon cans of vegetables with a butcher knife. We didn't have a mixer, nothing convenient there to work with.

We did some hard work, and my legs and feet would swell so bad sometime look like they's gone burst on me. Annie Mae contracted for sixty-five dollars a month, and mine was sixty dollars. They took out retirement, Social Security, and withholding. I *know* I wasn't getting minimum wage, but my husband was disabled to work.

**Interviewer:** *Do you think the movement did any good?*

Yes, because they didn't want us to vote. They did every way they could to keep the colored people from voting. We had to go to court down there in Oxford. I registered and I voted as long as I was able to go. I been voting ever since then. Now I vote absentee, and I have a tremble in my hand I can't write now. You know you suppose to stay inside that little circle . . . [Laughter.]

**Interviewer:** *How did you feel the first time you voted?*

I had pretty good nerves. I'm getting nervous right now, but I had good nerves. I felt good just to vote, I sure did.

**Interviewer:** *What have you done to stay in good health?*

You talking 'bout a Negro woman that's *worked*. I could hitch up a mule and plow just like a man. I have helped my daddy saw down trees in the spring and saw 'em up for stove wood, haul the blocks to the house, and bust them up. I have picked cotton, I have chopped cotton; I could pick over three hundred pounds of cotton when cotton was thick, and I always had my dinner. I have eaten good, home-raised solid food. I raised a good garden and have all kind of vegetables. We had our cows, we would milk cows, churn milk, had our own milk. Had a chicken house with a yard around it; we raised our chickens. I could kill a chicken whenever I got ready. We killed our meat, we put hogs up, penned the ones we gonna kill for meat and killed 'em. Had a big box, we salted them down for so many weeks, take them out the salt, hang 'em up, put a split through them, and in the early spring we's take that meat down, build a fire round a black wash kettle, and wash that meat off and put meat smoke on it. Then our hams we put them in sacks and tie them up and hang them back up. I didn't know nothing about going to the store buying ground beef or buying chickens or nothing till after my husband got down and we stop farming.

I'm on my own land now. We purchased one hundred acres of land through the FHA in 1943, and we paid for it in eight years. We had forty years to pay for it. We bought the land; it was twenty-five dollars an acre plus interest. We paid for the one hundred acres of land; we had a big red barn with a driveway through it. We grew corn, cotton, sorghum, peanuts, peas, sweet potatoes, and watermelons just for our use. We never sold nothing but cotton. We could borrow money to raise chickens if you wanted to, go into the chicken business; you could do that. Well, we had our own cows and hogs and things.

And I paid every penny on this house myself. I doubled up on my notes whenever I could, and we paid out the land, barn, and everything in eight years, and bought a used GMC truck cash. I wouldn't let Frank borrow money for clothes and things like that. I take my little money I make at school and buy the children's clothes, the little extra grocery, and stuff we was eating. That's why we paid out as quick as we did. I paid the last note when I got enough money saved to have what I call that little nest egg. The last payment I made was 2,700 and some dollars and a few cents; I still got my papers. And then I got my deed for this land thing. I paid out January 4th in '77, so I don't owe nobody.

**Interviewer:** *What is your secret for a long life?*

Do unto others as you like them to do unto you. Work hard. Try to be as independent as possible. I never been a beggar. Old as I am, I don't get no food stamps, I don't stand around these places for handouts. I have worked and God has blessed me. I was able; I have had good health all my days. I retired in '72 and I haven't been disabled to do for myself. And the supervisor was so well pleased at my work. I never have been a slacker. In what I do, I would do a good job of it. And I was lucky God have bless me. I can't help but praise him.

# Emmerline Robinson

## 1903–2006

Interviewed January 2004, Ashland, Mississippi, by Aviva Futorian, Roy DeBerry, and John Lyons

*Mrs. Robinson was 102 years young when she sat down with us and held court in her living room. The granddaughter of enslaved people, she heard first-person stories of the slave trade on her grandfather's lap. She lived for a brief while in St. Louis before returning to Benton County near the age of twenty, and she married soon after. Neither she nor her husband were active in the movement, a decision they were both firm on. "He didn't want to go out. That's the way it was." Several of her daughters and granddaughters were in her living room with us, helping to jog memories.*

◆ ◆ ◆

I would hear my grandparents speak about how they were sold. My grandfather was sold to the McKenzies. My daddy, grandfather, and great-granddaddy was on the roadside when this man comes by to buy the Negroes, you know? You know how people would buy people? For slaves? And if they had a horse, a mule or somethin' in the barn, they would destroy all of that. It was told to me, but I didn't get to see none of that.

When my father died, I was five years old. And Mama had to raise us eight children, four girls and four boys, she would go for work. Some years she had worked on shares, they called it. And she was a schoolteacher. She didn't have much to teach with. At that time, she had a horse and she had a woman's saddle. Sidesaddle. My mother would ride her horse sidesaddle when she'd go to teach school.

The first school I went to was a school near church named Shiloh, in Ashland, Mississippi. It was a plank building. That was my first school. Then after
my mother married, she moved down in the neighborhood of Spring Hill. I
was about thirteen. And so I went to Samuel's Chapel. I was learnin' to spell
pretty good at that time, and my 'rithmetic—I studied that mighty hard. That
was pretty good. And so, when I finished school, I stopped at the eighth grade.
I was capable of a teacher, but I never did try to teach. My mother's brother
was a principal and he would just have me to substitute sometimes.

Mother was tryin' to raise us eight children. It was just a plank old house.
We had two rooms. And I can remember one room where we had to cook and
eat. They had the two beds in the kitchen, one bed for the girls. And the parents
on the other side. And that's the way we lived a long time. After I got thirteen,
I had to work in the fields. Chopped cotton, picked cotton, and so on. I didn't
have much pleasure the children have now. I know that.

**Interviewer:** *Do you remember any racial violence in Benton County?*

It went on so bad. I can't tell where it all had happened. They went and got
some colored boys, two colored boys. They would lock some up and put 'em jail.
Keep 'em there so long. Couldn't get nothin' outta them. They took 'em down
'side of the road and they hung 'em. I didn't want to see any of it. It was awful,
you know. They never could prove who did all of this. I wasn't old enough to
consider, like I do now. I didn't have the feelings I . . . I know they were bad
to hang them boys. And they couldn't prove they did do it. We can't forget it.

◆  ◆  ◆

I had nine children. They all went to school until they grew up. Where did we
live? In a house that we had rented out. Later on, it had been a year, it got burnt
down. And we had to move back down to Springhill. And we lived down there
seventeen years in a wooden house. Wyatt Thomas's father's land.

**Interviewer:** *Do you remember when the civil rights workers came into Mississippi and to Benton County?*

Never did go to none of them meetings. Husband wouldn't allow it. If he didn't
want to go, I didn't want to go. He was lookin' out, you know? He didn't take
no part in it. He was just a common man. We were common farmin' people.
We made our livin' farmin'. And after he got disabled to farm, he went peddlin'
fish and peddlin' different stuff like that.

**Interviewer:** *Do you think things are better now in Benton County for people like you and your family than they were when you were growing up?*

[Laughs.] Is that a hard question? That's a hard question! Sometime I think it is and sometime I think it ain't. When King was here, he give us a chance to mix up. And *begged* us to mix up. But didn't we ever mix? Did we ever mix? That's the question. But it's been a big improvement, in some ways. Yes, it is.

# Mattie Jane Strickland

## 1913–2016

Interviewed September 2012, Ashland, Mississippi, by Aviva Futorian, Roy DeBerry, and John Lyons

*Ms. Strickland joined us for a conversation in her home off of Highway 4 in Ashland. Just shy of her one hundredth birthday, she was surrounded by relatives who deferred to her storytelling but aided her in recalling a date or name. She vividly recalled her childhood and teenage years in the 1910s and early '20s. Throughout the conversation, her deep faith, sense of humor, and love of her late husband, Felix, were evident. She ended our time together with a hymn, sung in a quiet, clear voice: "Jesus, keep me near the cross . . ."*

◆ ◆ ◆

Thomas MacDonald was my daddy. He farmed, was a sharecropper. Raised sorghum, raised corn, raised flowers. Everything he get, he raised it. And when we grew up big enough to plow, well then, he hollered for us to get the hoes. All the children got the hoes. Hoe cotton, hoe the sorghum patch, hoe the pea patch. We picked cotton. Daddy knew what to do, he'd get all the sacks. My sister and I would see how much could I pick a day, how much my little sister could pick a day. We had so far to walk to our school. I was pretty good size before Mama let me walk, especially in wintertime. Mama had to put me in a jacket, put me in gloves, just wrap me up good because we had to walk about three miles. I loved our teacher. We called her Ms. Fannie. Ms. Fannie Mason. She was patient with you. That's what I liked. She'd be forgiving, so you would understand.

It was all colored. I didn't wonder why. All I knew was, that's just school. I wasn't thinking nothing about, "Why was this and why was that?" I just went to school, you know? I wasn't thinking about how different it ought to have been.

◆ ◆ ◆

Felix, I met him at church, I remember that. This particular night, they had a something like a concert. And I was young. I wasn't about to call myself courting. No, no, no. But this boy, he tried to slip around and talk to me. Mama didn't care. She let me start talking to him after I got about fifteen, going on sixteen. When that age come, and I got old enough, she told us, "You go to church, you can talk. But the boy better know how to talk to you." I just liked his ways. You know, some boys looked like they got too much mouth. But the one I married, I liked him. Because when he'd come up to you, he would speak to you right. And when we'd go to church, I'd always sing in the choir. I'd look out at the door, he'd be standing there.

**Interviewer:** *Did he ask your father if he could marry you?*

No, I'm going to tell you the truth. He didn't ask Papa, he didn't ask Mama. He asked *me*. And, that night, after we got everything wrapped up and ready, I then walked out there and got in the car with him. We went and got married. We didn't ask Mom and Pop or nothing.

He was living with his mother and father. They was renting. That's where we farmed. We used to raise a big sorghum crop. And my husband would have a good garden. I would cook. Greens, cabbage, peas, hanging peas, all like that, you know? Different stuff that you had to go to the garden to get. Daddy would always raise his hogs. And Mama would raise her chickens. Had plenty of eggs. If we were going to kill chickens, we'd put up four or five in a pen and feed them. And then we'd kill them. Wring their neck off. They would; I couldn't do it. My girl did it.

You don't want to know how many children I had! [Laughs.] Eight children. Oh yes, I was a *woman*.

I was worried about them being treated right. You know, when they were going out there.

**Interviewer:** *And today, you're on your own land. How did you get it?*

People that I know. [Laughs.]

**Interviewer:** *Did you ever think of moving?*

No. Because I was raised here all of my life. My daddy and mother raised us here. And so I just love it, that's all I can say. People always have treat us right. We always have got along with these people. And so I just love to stay here.

**Interviewer:** *What do you attribute to your long life?*

I eat peas. I eat peas, cabbage, butter beans, mashed potatoes. And I'm going to tell you the truth. All it calls for is to treat a person right.

# Nan Gibson

## 1923–2006

Interviewed November 2004, Lamar, Mississippi, by Aviva Futorian, Roy DeBerry, and John Lyons

*For over sixty-five years, Nan Gibson was a housekeeper and caretaker for the Farese family, a prominent white family of lawyers in Benton County who many in the movement viewed with suspicion. The Farese family patriarch, John Farese, was a native of Massachusetts who came to Mississippi for school, got a law degree, and settled in Benton County. They were heavily involved in both local and state politics. Due to her relationship with the Farese family, she herself was viewed with suspicion by many people active in the movement.*

◆ ◆ ◆

As far as I know, my parents were born and reared right here in Benton County. They were sharecroppers. We was up at daylight out in the field picking cotton, pulling corn.

We didn't get shoes until Christmas time, you know, only one pair of shoes. My granddaddy, pretty close to Christmas time, he would come and say he going to settle up today. He'd come home and say, "I didn't clear anything, but get your shoe sizes and come back."

Wyatt Thomas's daddy, my grandfather's boss, he would tell my granddaddy to get our shoe size and I guess he'd taken him somewhere and bought them. You know, put it on the book for the next year. They used to sell chickens and eggs and buy our schoolbooks. I remember that when we needed some books they'd tell us, "Go to the hen house and see if there's some eggs," and we'd go and take some and sell them and try to get that book.

Frankly, I got to about the eighth or ninth grade. My grandparents taught us to work. We had to work for a living. And if you were smart and looked pretty decent, you know, people would come for you to help them. I worked at a café in Ashland, and Mr. Farese[4] would always come down to eat every Friday afternoon. They'd come down and they'd eat dinner that night. And with me being a worker there, would serve them.

I'm eighty now, and I worked for him about sixty-five years. Everything— cooked, washed, ironed, cleaned house, take care of the kids. When I first started working for him, they want to know if I had registered to vote. I had not. And he said, "Well, I want you to." He impressed me that being a citizen you need to be registered where you can vote. He said, "I'm going to help you." And he did. They give you something and you had to interpret it. And he know what they were going to give out. He would give me, what they was going to give us to study.

I got harassed when I went in to register. In 1943, I remember that because I had such a hard time when I went up there to vote. There wasn't anybody in the office but the clerk[5] and in less than five minutes there were so many people and they were talking loud and trying to distract me. Talking so loud. Then, if you didn't get it right, you wouldn't pass.

**Interviewer:** *What made you decide to want to vote? Did you follow politics at the time?*

Well, he [John Farese] was in politics and I think that was one of the reasons that he was interested in people being qualified to vote, and that would be a help to him.

**Interviewer:** *He named his son after the person who assassinated Abraham Lincoln. Did you ever wonder about that?*

I think about it often. I don't know, I don't know, I don't know . . . I guess that he was trying to be, be in with both parties, you know. Some of the whites didn't like it [voter registration], and he wanted to be on their side. He wanted to help the black, but he didn't want the white to know it. I guess that's the way it was.

**Interviewer:** *What did you think when the civil rights movement became strong here?*

I know we needed it and it helped us a lot. I know it has. Black people have been able to get good jobs and I think they were encouraged to go to school and I think a lot of doors was open where they had been closed. Getting loans to go to college which they never was before. That helped a lot. As far as going to the meeting and things, no. My own people made smart remarks to me about working for the Fareses, they called me Ms. Farese. I worked for the Fareses, to take care of their kids. They were in and out the legislature, and my daughter had to have welfare help with her, and I was afraid that if I went with them [to the meetings], that little check would be cut off. I'm coming straight now.

**Interviewer:** *What do you think he thought about school integration?*

That I will never know. I do know when we got President Kennedy elected. He says, "Now we got the right president in there to help you." I remember him saying that. Like I said, I think he was trying to play both sides. In fact, I know he was from what I'm hearing. Because he always treated me as I was one of the family, you know. And his kids still do today. He was from the North, and he knew they didn't like northerners. When he first came, they treated him— his kids was misused and neglected in school. The girl come home many days crying, saying they called her "Yankee." So he knew what it took to get along with them, and he played it on both sides.

I had problems with the Ku Klux Klan. I'm the first black to have a, a FHA brick home. Mr. Farese helped me to get it, my loan and everything. I don't know who did it, but they castrated dogs and left a knife there when they were building my house. Somebody resented me getting a brick house. [Mr. Farese] had the law to come out there and get the prints off of the knife. Whoever they thought it was, I never was told. I think it was because they didn't want Negroes to have that property. And I got it and built the house on it. When it was night and I had to come home, they would be on the corner, but I just made up my mind I would honk the horn, and if you don't get out of my way, I'm going to run you over. They meddled at me for a long time. And they meddled at me until they decided I wasn't going to pay them any attention. And they just quit.

**Interviewer:** *Do you think things are better now?*

We get better pay and have opportunity now to work in banks and offices. And me now, I feel just as comfortable [with white people] as I do with my people. I could have then, with them, but now if I go in a café or get on a bus, I don't feel like we always got to sit on the back of the bus.

## Chapter 6

# SERVICE

*A postmaster, a deputy sheriff, an educator, a politician, and two Vietnam veterans were among those we interviewed. Their stories are larger than their jobs, but their professions, most of them unlikely, have played a large part of determining who they are. Without discounting the personal achievements of the following interviewees, much of their success is a tangible result of the movement.*

# James "Bubba" Griffin

## Born 1957

Interviewed November 2014, Ashland, Mississippi, by Aviva Futorian and John Lyons

*Mr. Griffin was the first black person elected District 2 supervisor, a position he has held for over two decades. After his father passed away prematurely, he was raised by his mother. His wiry frame belies his energy and entrepreneurial spirit. In addition to holding elected office, he also manages a convenience store, several rental properties, and a landscaping business. What motivates him? "God gives some people something and you don't know why. I don't know why. I don't want my mom, in her last years, to have to do things she would never want to do. She's taken care of." We met with him in his convenience store before he brought us to his home, where we talked.*

◆ ◆ ◆

I know what poor is all about. My family *invented* the word poor. Two families lived in the same three-room house. We raised our own meat, had our own gardens. We had to go to a spring to get water. I remember there was no bathroom, no running water, no nothing like that. Everything was from the spring to the house. After I got of age, then I realized that we were poor. But while I was in this position and I saw nothing different, then you don't know you're poor. But I never went hungry. Never. No.

**Interviewer:** *As a little boy, what made you realize that there are black people and there are white people, and they are different?*

Keep in mind when you're reared, you're sharecropping, you stayin' on somebody else's place. When that person comes out and your folks went out there, the first thing they did was their head went *down*. You couldn't look them in the face, you couldn't look at them in the eye.

I could only say, "Why?" Mama, she didn't have the words to explain it. She just says, "You don't do that. You don't question them, you don't go through the front door. Even if you play with the kids, you play in the backyard." Right now that's why I'm interested in history. To say, "Why? Where this come from, how this happen?" We all supposed to be one group of human beings. How could one be a lower status than others? We all bleed alike, we share things alike. How could you do all the things together after school—work together, chop cotton together, picked cotton together. But there is a separating that happens in education and knowledge? Because knowledge is power.

◆ ◆ ◆

**Interviewer:** *When you started school, it was the all-black school?*

All-black. Teachers all-black, principal, everybody is all-black. Didn't know about [Freedom of Choice]. Well, if my mom knew about it, you know, when you live on somebody's place you tend to do what they tell you to do. You see what I'm saying? If he told you're not going there, you didn't go there.

**Interviewer:** *You feel you were being deprived?*

Yes. When you leaving a shack and going to a house, you know it's different. When we left my house and went to the guy that my mom worked for, you could see the transition. So, you knew, if his kid is going to another school, it *had* to be a better school. Everything was laid out for the other race more so they were for us.

I went to the integrated school in ninth grade, graduated in 1976. When we went to Ashland High School, it was only a few whites left there. They went to Hickory Flat. It was like being in the black school, but we just had white teachers and the white principal. The Stewards and other families had already made an initial appearance at Ashland. They'd laid the foundation, but you can tell the tension was still there.

Now that's how I look at it—we were better off at the black school because we had caring teachers. They understood you. If there was a child that was slow-learning, the black teacher was more caring and considerate of them. For example, I remember not being taught anything about education because my parents didn't have enough education to help me with education. So, now you don't have a head start. We have to go from home and get in an environment to talk about learning. And all we knew how to do, from age zero to six, all we knew how to do is play and *work*. So now you hand me a book and tell me, "You've got to learn your ABCs." It is sort of like teaching a person a different language.

So, my first couple of years in first and second grade was a hard deal. It wasn't so much about the books being outdated. I mean, we probably had old books, but who knew? It don't matter what kind of book you have. If you don't get the foundation, the book is no good. I think the foundation was better, I think the educational level was better, at the predominantly black school. Sometimes what you think you want is not best for you. Sometimes I think the transition might have hurt us as a group of people. Because we lost our identity in the transition. Because the black teacher would tell you, "I am going to talk to your parent." They knew each other. It took a whole community to raise a family. They'd go to your house to communicate. While the white teacher wouldn't go in your household and communicate to a parent about your condition, what you're doing. So we lost a lot of that connection.

The white teachers, they felt that you should know it. They didn't want you to be there. They would teach you because the law said they *got* to teach you. And if you force a man do a thing against his will, he won't be as aggressive and as fair with you.

**Interviewer:** *Were there any white teachers that weren't like that?*

Ms. Renick was one of them, she was a math teacher. She came from the poor side of a white people's family. She was very fair. She cared, she'd pinch your ear and get you do the work. Kids catch on quick, can sense when you don't care. They [white students] got preference, yeah, they got preference. You got angry, you talked about among the students, but we soon you talk down because, what are you going to do? You go home to your mom and dad, you go to the principal, what you going to do?

**Interviewer:** *Did you ever hear from older black students who were there before you?*

They say it was hostile. Students that graduated before we did, they say it was all hostile. Fights broke out, you know, white-black fights. The only thing they tell you, "You got to fight for yourself. Fight for yourself, don't let them walk over you. Don't let the teacher walk over you." And then the older black kids, they told us, "Speak up. Don't put your head down when talk you to them." That's the one thing the older kids taught us: *Don't look down.*

◆ ◆ ◆

I knew when I graduated I was going to college. I knew that. I wanted that knowledge. I say knowledge is power. You cannot defeat anything if you haven't knowledge about the thing. And so, I pursued, went to Northwest Community College, then went to Ole Miss on a minority scholarship, then went to University of Memphis and worked on a master's for a while. Then I got into politics.

I will never forget 1987. Somebody broke into my little store[1] when I was at school and stole some stuff. And I know the guy who did it. Everybody told me go to the justice of the peace and have papers taken out on him. Well, since this guy's family is a big family, he [the justice of the peace] wouldn't let me take an affidavit. He refused to let me take an affidavit. And so I talked to some of my friends in college and they said, "The election is next year—you run against him. Start now." So, my friends in college got to pool our resources and money. And we bought posters and we begin to motivate the young people.

**Interviewer:** *And who was the guy you ran against?*

Jimmy Carpenter, white guy. He had been in office for I think three terms. And his dad said, "Ain't no way that nigger beats my son in an election." So, we strategized and said we'll get the young vote. You know, I would at the end, and they, the whites, kept sayin', "He ain't gonna beat him, he ain't gonna beat him." So they got comfortable. So we kept on. We'd go in a black house, if we didn't get the parents, we got the children. Our strategy was, if you don't get the parent, we go to the kids. Sell our idea to them. And we did, we did. See, it wasn't to win. It was just to have a good number to show. We had no idea we were going to win because I'd never been in politics before, never did anything in politics. Hadn't voted but one time in my whole life.

But I couldn't get my mom. She was worried and said, "They are going to kill you." Lord knows, she didn't want me to run. And it was a close election. I think I beat him by one hundred twenty-five votes. When I got elected, she couldn't believe it. Mama was ecstatic about it and everything was great. And it was a little shock throughout the whole county, you know. The main thing it did was say to young blacks: "Go and vote, you need to go vote." 'Cause they made the transition.

I've been a supervisor twenty-two years. Whatever you want in your district you're responsible for it. If you see there's a need of a housing, if it is water, if the sewage, whatever you can get with grants. You are the governor of your district. When I got elected, I made it a point that I had keep the workforce equal. I have white guys, black guys. Maybe it will make a difference.

I saw a white lady the other week. She's maybe seventy and her granddaughter's got a mixed baby. And she's refused to let it live in the house. She told me that. I said, "This is your blood. You *know* she's your granddaughter." Now we can call each other, she talks to me, we express our own views on things. She's a nice person. But how could she say that? She says, "I don't care. I don't want her in my house." I said, "You're gonna die with that in your heart?" She said, "If I have to." You look at her, you won't even believe she'd make a statement like that. But she did. And she was serious about it.

To me, that's deep. That's deep. Racism is still alive and well in Benton County. Because we won't let it die. It will if they let it. It will die. But they won't let it. King said it very well. We shouldn't be judged by the color of our skin but the content of our character. What's in your heart, what you believe, what knowledge you have. That's what you judge me about: my *knowledge*, not the color of my skin.

**Interviewer:** *When do you think that will happen?*

When Jesus comes back.

# Joe Batts

## Born 1950

Interviewed September 2013, Lamar, Mississippi, by Aviva Futorian Roy DeBerry, and John Lyons

*A deputy sheriff of Benton County, Joe Batts is a veteran of the US Army, daycare owner, counselor at a Tennessee Corrections facility, hunter, and farmer. His older brother, Clay, was very active in the civil rights movement before he died in a swimming accident in Wisconsin in the mid-1960s. A quiet, reserved man, Joe was heavily influenced by Clay. He is also extremely self-deprecating. He'll conclude our talk by saying, with a smile, "I hope you didn't find me as boring as I find myself." The following conversation took place under a peach tree in his front yard.*

◆ ◆ ◆

We farmed our own land. The land originally came from my mother's father, Henry Jackson. I cannot remember what's on the deed, but it was farmed back in the 1800s. Don't know the history of it. But I do know that my grandfather, in addition to farming, he also ran a small store. So I'm sure that that's how he managed to start getting some of the money to purchase the land. When I was younger, we moved to another farm a mile or so from here. Over there, we did I guess you would call it sharecropping, plus working this piece of property too. Just so that we'd have more land to work. It provided a little bit of extra income.

One of the things that I remember was that whenever we had to be on Highway 5, we'd try not to be there around three thirty to four, because of the buses. At that time, when school buses passed by, if they (I'm talking about white kids) saw a black kid on the road, you could expect to get yelled at and thrown at and everything else. It's just one of those situations. It was . . . I don't know, it wasn't intimidating. But it's just one of those things where you try to avoid. I knew that there was racial prejudice, but it never bothered me because my family didn't talk about that very much. One of the things that I'm proud of about my father and my family is that they didn't hold grudges against anybody or anything. And I guess we were kind of brought up the same way. Later on, after the civil rights movement started, I was a little bit older and there were more activities going on while we lived in the house over on Meridian Road. I remember one morning, we found a cross burnt in the yard. I'm sure that it was just one of the spin-offs of the civil rights movement. In addition to that, Clay being several years older than me, he was active in the movement, and I'm sure that had a lot to do with it. Clay was . . . well, he was my brother and I loved him and he loved me. And generally, as siblings go, we all got along well. Once I got older, I started having more interactions with him, and he impressed me. He was determined, foremost, to get an education. And he had decided he was going to law school. I know he would've done that, and I'm sorry he didn't get to fulfill that dream. Because I think he would've been a doggone good lawyer, I really do. But, from the people whom I talked to, who knew him, they all respected him. I just have not heard any bad comments about Clay.

Back then, some of the white landowners, and some who were not landowners, were in intimidation mode, trying to nip this thing in the bud. And during that period of time, my father got really concerned, particularly about the boys, because you just didn't want them to get into situations which could be dangerous. We got the general safety lecture. "Don't do anything that would cause people to target you for any reason." You could tell that my father was really uptight, but he was not the one to say, "You don't go to civil rights meetings," because he generally wanted us to participate. But yet, he was not one of those people who had an in-your-face attitude. He was pretty mild. I remember when I first started school and started talking about being bullied. He said, "Don't ever go out and start a fight. If you're getting bullied, tell your teachers about it. If they stop it, fine. But if they don't, do it yourself. And if you get into a fight, you make the other guy know he doesn't want to do that again." And so I just kind of followed that advice all my life. And that was really kind of attitude that my father had. He didn't want to infringe on anybody else's rights. And he was not a very verbal guy, I guess—kind of like me. But he had a lot of backbone, even for a quiet person.

**Interviewer:** *So at what point did you start attending an integrated school?*

It was the tenth grade, I believe. Attending Ashland High, it was my own decision. And my folks said, "If you want to go, then go." Probably one of the reasons was that Clay had gone. And the other is that, I knew a number of other students were going and I thought it was important that black students went. So I counted myself in that number. And I think it was a year prior to that, I found out a little bit about the disparity between the white school and the black school from one simple fact. When I was in eighth grade, we went to algebra for the first time and we had two algebra books at Old Salem, and those were two that our instructor, Mr. William Henley, scrounged from somewhere. We weren't given any by the county. And that very next year, I started working on a summer program for the county and I worked around the [white] school. And in working around the school, I went to one of the storage houses because we have to clean out some of the storage buildings. And there was *stacks* of algebra books, the same type that we were using and only had two of them, stacks in the storage shop there in Ashland. And for them, those were castoff books, they had new books. We were using an edition of their old books, but only had two of them when there was stacks of them there in the storage building there at the high school.

I was one of those kids I guess you would call a nerd or a bookworm. I was not very outgoing. I'm not very outgoing now, not a very social being. One of the things that I like to do was read. Generally, if you like to read the subject matter, it evolves on you. The more you study it, the deeper you get into it and the more interesting it is. It was that way in Ashland and in Old Salem, too. So, I don't think things were very much more challenging in Ashland than it was at Old Salem other than the tension, the social thing.

It was different going to a school with white kids and having white teachers because before then, I hadn't really associated with whites. You encountered the normal amount of bullying, but there were a few thuggish actors too. And through it all, I guess I kind of fell back on my father's advice, "Don't start anything." Fortunately, I never got into any physical confrontations. When I went there, along with several others, there wasn't anything that we held back from. If there was something that we wanted to participate in, we participated. And we just tried to make a full school experience of it. And sometimes you would hear remarks that you weren't supposed to hear. When you tend to reach a point where you're almost comfortable, some of these remarks that would be said, that were supposedly out of your hearing, they'd come up. And it kind of let you know . . . I was in English class and I sat next to the door and I heard my teacher remark to another teacher, "That nigger made the highest grade in the class again," which . . . what can I say? It didn't bother me. But I was kind of surprised to hear it from the teacher. I'm sure if she had known that I was listening, she wouldn't've said it. But it's just that kind of thing.

**Interviewer:** *How'd you decide to attend Ole Miss?*

It wasn't for any great social reason. It had a good reputation. Number two, it was a state school, which meant it cost less than private schools. And number three, it was closer to home than Jackson State or some of the other colleges. Because one of the things that I wanted to do was to be able to help my father here on the farm. He was getting older, and I was the last son. And so my intentions were to be close enough to help him out with what he needed. And Ole Miss to me seemed a logical choice. Being on a college campus was a culture shock, just like many other things are when you're doing it for the first time. The predominant feeling that I was having was: "I'm probably not wanted here." During my first fall there, we were coming back across campus after a football game. We were riding around on pickup trucks. We're waving football flags, yelling football stuff, and another pickup truck drove up to us. And they pulled out shotguns and told us, "Niggers, go home!" But the other feeling was, "I've got something to do and I need to get it done, whether I'm wanted or not." You just go on and do what you got to do.

◆ ◆ ◆

After I graduated, I went into the army and well, I kind of enjoyed it. It just so happened that I started to get a few good breaks, which I messed up because of, I guess, ignorance. Back then, the army was offering some of the better students an opportunity to get a pilot's license while in college. And I turned that down because I didn't want to be committed to four years in the army, okay? I was offered an ROTC scholarship, which would have paid for my schooling, but again, I turned it down because I didn't want to be committed for four years in the army. They offered to send me back to school for a master's degree, full salary, fully paid, and I turned that down because again, I didn't know if I want to stay around that long. So twenty years later, I just look back on all of the opportunities that I turned down, trying to avoid that four-year commitment.

When I got there [Germany], the unit that I went to was in the midst of a what was called REFORGER. It's an acronym that came from "Return of Forces to Germany." That's the annual exercise that they were having at that time in which the US forces had exercises with the German units. It meant that there were military units running around all over Germany doing military exercises. I guess it was a good experience, but it was kind of tough too because at that time, there were a lot of emphasis on the nuclear weapons. My unit was nuclear capable, so it was a lot of work involved.

The second time I was there, I was the deputy commander of a small military post in a little town down in the southern part of Germany. Now, that was a good assignment. I liked that. One of my duties was to, I guess, reinforce German relations. So I get all of the invitations to the parties and the beer fests and things of that nature, and that was good. I enjoyed that. Really friendly community.

**Interviewer:** *There were a lot of white people under your command.*

The military is based on rank and if you got the rank, you got the authority. There were situations in which, I won't say, preferences were made, but sometimes when it came to getting various assignments, I was one of the last ones to get them. But overall, I think it was great. Our leadership was good. They awarded you for what you did, not for who you were. I enjoyed that.

I had one incident that was kind of funny. When I was commanding the unit, I had a mess sergeant who for some reason just could not get his act together. When we go out, we'd take the full unit, everything with us. In order to get started, you needed an early breakfast. And for some reason, he just could not seem to get it done. He was a horrible cook, food would be burned, he could not get stuff done on time, and I called him into my office. I started talking to him about it, and one of the things that he came out with was, he said it just wasn't fair. I said, "What isn't fair?" He says, "Here I am a white man, and you're a black man and you got me standing in front of your desk." I just said, "You know, I'm the captain, you're a sergeant. You messed up." And that was when I got him shipped out, not because of that comment. The comment didn't bother me. But the problem was, he was slowing my unit down. He was not doing what he needed to do. It surprised me. It really did. But what can I say? It happens and I guess out of the experiences I've had, I've kind of learned not to be surprised by a lot of things.

**Interviewer:** *So you came back, after being gone for twenty years, to Benton County. What changes did you notice?*

I really expected just to see some of the old southern attitudes that were prevalent when I left, and I didn't see a lot of that when I came back. People were pretty much accepting each other as such on the surface. Now, you know that beneath the surface, there are going to be undertones that are still going to be there. But there were interracial couples here when I got back. I didn't expect to see that. Starting the job that I have now, I got a lot of warm comments from people of both races. That was really good to see.

I drifted around for couple of months. Unfortunately, my mother passed. When she did, I told my father I'd come back and spend a few months with him until he got reoriented. After that, every time I started to leave, he got all

Benton County Deputy Sheriff Joe Batts. Courtesy of Aviva Futorian.

down, so I wound up staying. I just looked at the climate around here, and one of the things that I saw was that there were a number of high school students, girls, who were having kids and didn't have any place to put them. Some were dropping out of school. And so one of the things that I set out to do was to set up a daycare in Benton County. So actually, I started the first licensed daycare center here in Benton County. I ran it for about eight years.

Then, I went to work for Harlan County Corrections in Tennessee as a counselor. I worked there for about two years and that was another educational experience. It's dangerous, to say the least—both for the employees and for the prisoners because of the things that go on there. I went to work there in I think it was November 2002, if I recall correctly. And about two months later, I was put into a unit that housed most of the gang units. And just before I got there, that same unit had just killed a counselor. They stabbed him 101 times, that unit. Yeah, they threw me in there [laughs], which was kind of funny. Then, I started work for the Sheriff's Department in Benton County. My father had gotten to a point where he was really ill and he needed someone around that could respond quickly. So I was determined to move closer to home, working. I was still living here, but I was working thirty miles away. So, I started lookin' around for a job, and one of the county supervisors, Bubba Griffin, told me that there was an opening at the Sheriff's Department, and I talked to the sheriff and signed up right there.

One of the things that I like about the job—you do have an opportunity to help people and to talk to them. And I think that's great, one of the rewards of having the job. This is going to sound strange, but I don't like arrestin' people. I really don't. I do it quite often and I have to do it. But, if there's a situation that I can resolve without taking somebody to jail, I will do that. And there's some times when you have to do some very distasteful things in very distasteful situations. People unfortunately get killed one way or another. Sometimes it's by accident. Sometimes it's by murder. And working those kind of things gets to be kind of hard. And the hard part about that mainly is looking at the grief that the families are put through in those situations. That's just real tough.

**Interviewer:** *You ever think about running for sheriff?*

It's just that at this point, I don't think it'll . . . I don't think I want to do that. One reason, I'm getting old. And right now, I'm in excellent health, but I'm sixty-three now. But, by the time of the next election, if I were to be elected, I'd be sixty-six, and somehow I don't know if . . . well, I don't want to tie myself down to serve four years.

**Interviewer:** *You said the same thing about the army—*

You're right! And I thought about that many times. But you're right. And tell you the truth, there's still a year or so before you have to qualify to run. I guess I could still change my mind, yeah. The sheriff does not have to do some of the things that his deputies do. He doesn't have to work the hours as his deputy has to work, but still has to put up with the headaches. I love to hunt, I do some farming. I grow a little bit of corn for the freezer. I raise a few cows, simply because I just like to see calves. I have some horses because I used to love to ride horses. And I intend to get back into it. I don't know, I just love horses. Horses are better than blood pressure medicine.

**Interviewer:** *You think young people have a sense of how amazing it is to have a black man as a deputy sheriff in Benton County?*

Quite frankly, I don't know whether they should think it's amazing or not. Because if you look at the fact that all of us should have the opportunity to do those types of things, it shouldn't be amazing. If you look at the past, in light of things that have happened within our lifetime, it would be very unusual. As for me, I would never have thought we would have seen a black president in my lifetime. I just didn't expect that to happen, but it did. One of the things that I think is lost is that many black kids are forgetting that whenever they do things, they need to put their best foot forward rather than being willing to just slouch along at something, and still think that they're entitled to the best that life has to offer. We have some white kids that do the same thing. I wish both black and white could have a better perspective of what this country has gone through in the last sixty years, and where it has come from.

# Charlie Walls

## Born 1949

Interviewed September 2012, Ashland, Mississippi, by Aviva Futorian, Roy DeBerry, and John Lyons

*The second of fourteen children, Charlie Walls is the son of sharecropping parents. He moved to Memphis, Tennessee, after graduating from Old Salem School in 1968. He was then promptly drafted into the Vietnam War. Despite numerous health problems—including hearing loss, a deteriorating spine, and confirmed exposure to Agent Orange in the war—he is among the friendliest and most optimistic people with whom we've talked. He sat down with us in his home off of Highway 4, just outside the town of Ashland.*

◆ ◆ ◆

My family sharecropped. And I was old enough to get a little part of that. What I mean is that I was old enough to work in the fields, plow mules, and just help do what I was told to do. Sharecropping was like your parents work on someone's place, a plantation or what have you. The owner gets half of the profit and the family is supposed to get half of the profit, but it really didn't work like that. At the end of the year, they used to call it "settling up time." I didn't really know what the definition of "settling up" was, but I know we used to look for a little money at the end of the year, and most of the time we didn't get any. Our parents would go meet with the owner and when they would come back they would say we didn't get any money this year, because he said we owed him all the money we were supposed to get.

Mr. Robert Bonds, a white man, was the landowner. You know, he was good to the family, he was really. But I'm speaking in terms of money and that was the only way we had of getting clothes, getting shoes and food. I can remember we used to raise gardens and go hunting for rabbits, squirrels, and all that kind of stuff. I can remember that very clearly. That's how we ate.

We used to what they called "catch up." They paid you by the hundred pounds.[2] We got one dollar and a half a hundred, sometimes it would be two dollars a hundred. I had a grandmother, she would be pulling three sacks. She would make us get in front of her and she would tell us, "Don't let me catch you!" And she meant it, so we had to move to stay out of her way. Meanwhile, we was picking a lot of cotton, two rows at the same time. I used to pick 300 hundred pounds. We had to get money enough to go around.

You asked, "How did I pass the time?" Well, by bending over, picking cotton and putting it in a sack! [Laughter] That's how the time passed.

◆ ◆ ◆

I went to Greenwood Church School until I got to third grade. I was in the third grade when I started Old Salem. I don't see how we made it through school. I really don't, because we didn't go as much as I thought we should have. Back then, they used to keep us out of school during harvesting time. We had to stay out and help harvest the crop, and then we would go to school. The time that we did go, we had to buckle down and study hard to be able to pass to the next grade. When you're sharecropping, school didn't exist as far as the owner was concerned. The number one priority was getting those crops harvested. They don't care what it took, you either do that or you move off the place.

At the time I was around ten, they had the white bathroom, the black bathroom, they had the white water fountain, they had the black water fountain. I can remember very well in Ashland they had a doctor's office, Dr. Gray. The whites went in the front and the blacks went in the back, and never come across each other in his office. And we grew up, you know, in that environment. I thought it was awful, I did. I really couldn't accept it as being okay. But my parents feared the situation. You're living on a white man's place. He owns everything, you got to do what he say. I was old enough to realize Momma and Daddy had to do what the white man say, or we would have to go try to look for a home, and it wasn't no homes around then. They had to do the best they could, and that meant doing what the white man say, nothing different.

**Interviewer:** *Did your parents ever go to any civil rights meetings?*

Yeah, they did. But back then parents didn't tell you their business. As a child, you wasn't allowed to know what was going on between grown people, so we had to respect that. And it's a lot of things children know now we didn't know as a child because they didn't allow us to know it. They was scared. They were scared for the civil rights, because at that time the Ku Klux Klan used to come through the neighborhood at night shooting their guns in the air, blowing the car horns, blinking the lights. Just a line of them come through. They used to burn crosses, you know, put them in the ground and set them afire. Everybody was scared to death. My parents were, too.

◆ ◆ ◆

The movement was all about giving us freedom and the right to pick and choose where we wanted to go. Who we wanted to associate with and to bring blacks and whites together, that's what I felt it was all about. Bringing blacks and whites together. We knew that was taking place, and I guess the most fearful thing was, how was it gonna be for the first ones to go to Ashland School? Ashland was where all the whites went and Old Salem is where all the blacks were. Nobody in our class had nerves enough to do that. So we all said we gonna stay at Old Salem and graduate together. And that's what we did. In 1968, we graduated together.

After I graduated, I was offered a job in Memphis at a place called the Memphis Furniture Factory, so I worked there until Momma called me and told me that I had a letter. I need to come home and see about it. So I went home, and they gave me a schedule when I need to report back to Memphis to be inducted into the US Army. So I left August 4, 1969, to take my basic training. And in December, I had to go to Vietnam. The war was still hot. In fact, the reason we had to go in such a hurry is because the plane they carried over before we went, they had lost almost all of them in the war. We were a replacement. In other words, if one crew gets killed, they send another crew over to take their place. I was scared to death—scared to death. And the worst thing was, when we landed over in Ben Guerir Air Force Base, the stewardess gave us a little speech. Said that "we will see y'all next year at this time." At that time, everybody was just thinking, "We got to stay over here a whole year without seeing our families and everybody." And we knew once we were over there, wasn't no coming back until your time was up, if you was blessed enough to make it through it. I was more or less a "to myself" person. I just kept my mind on my family, hoping in the good Lord that I get out of this alive, you know? Just doing what I was told so I could get out and get back home.

We had a sergeant that told us it wasn't no colors in the military. It was one color—military green. Wasn't no black, white, brown. It wasn't no different color. He said we are all as one and we got to think like that and be like that in order to survive. And really it drawed everybody close together. My best friend in the military was white. It really was. And even when I got out of Vietnam and came back to the States, I had three white guys that practically helped me raised my little daughter. I'm quite sure the white guys that was my friends, it's probably their first time associating with a black. But then, *everybody* was scared, you know? When everybody's got their freedom to do what you want, everybody's got a habit of taking and choosing their own lifestyle. But if you're under the gun, so to speak, where everybody's got to do the same thing, you don't have any choice but to be as one. The military will do that to you. The military really brought a lot of people together.

I stayed over there about six months. I had a kidney stop functioning, so they had to rush me out of Vietnam and send me to Camp Zama, Japan, to have a kidney surgery. After I had the kidney surgery, they sent me back to Fort Campbell, Kentucky, to serve the rest of my time in the military. I lost part of my hearing. The VA just do not do what they pretend they do as far as taking care of veterans. They do not. I was exposed to Agent Orange. It was good a thing that they done, they did tell me. And they took the blame for that, but I'm at the point now where it's been almost two years and they haven't done anything about it.

**Interviewer:** *How did you end up back in Benton County?*

When I was younger, I wanted to hurry up and grow up so I could go up north. Because it seemed like, to us as a family, the ones up north was making a lot of money. They were practically rich. They used to come down to visit sometimes, they drove fancy cars and you know, the North seemed like it was the place to go. After I become a man and learned a little bit about the world, I just didn't want to live up north.

Memphis was the place where everybody wanted to go. We were having good times, good jobs. It was convenient and all that good stuff, but when I came back [from the army] it wasn't the same Memphis. Friends used to tell me that the street we lived on wasn't the same. It was a lot of killing, stealing, just wasn't safe. In that short amount of time, it was totally different. I just couldn't take a chance on raising a child in that kind of environment. So I put in to have an FHA house built, and it passed through. We bought a mobile home to live temporarily until we got this house. Once they approve, you don't get the house right then. It may be a year or two years later. So we lived in a mobile home right out front there until they got the house built and that was in '77.

**Interviewer:** *What do you like about staying here?*

Freedom. The country is just my life—peaceful and quiet. You got a choice to raise your own food, to have little garden and stuff. I'm an outdoors person anyway. I just love space, to where I can expand and do what I want to do. I feel like I own this and this is my life.

◆ ◆ ◆

We still have some prejudice or racial situations. A lot of it is under the cover now. It is just not out in the open. Integration really busted the bubble. I mean, it really drawed a lot of people closer together. So I feel like it's a lot better than what I had in life as far as being able to get a better education, go to college, and this kind of stuff. You got to put forth all your effort to get the best education you can get, because everything has advanced to another level as far as electronics, computers—which didn't exist, you know, through most of our life. Now things are where you just can't survive without education. You can't.

# Jimmie Cathey

## Born 1949

Interviewed April 2007, Holly Springs, Mississippi, by Aviva Futorian, Roy DeBerry, and John Lyons

*Jimmie Cathey desegregated Ashland in the tenth grade. Although he was kicked out of Ashland, he later finished high school in Tippah County, went to college, and earned a master's degree in education, before spending a career in the US Post Office. He rose through the ranks and served as the OIC (officer in charge) in Ashland's post office, then left Benton County to become the postmaster in Valley Park near Vicksburg. He then became the customer service analyst for the Mississippi District. He then served as postmaster for Ackerman before returning to Benton County to become postmaster in Michigan City. He was also an assistant appraiser for the Marshall County tax assessor official in Holly Springs. He's also a veteran of the Vietnam War.*

◆ ◆ ◆

My grandfather walked all the way from North Carolina down to this area. The name Cathey came about as a name that was given to him by slave owners. He was a slave there. I think somebody from this area bought him and they came down here. At that time, it was a situation where if you were a good person, then your slave owner would give you some land. And so, as the slave owners were getting up in age, then they started giving land to some of the "good" slaves that they owned. And in addition to that, then there were my parents and grandparents' parents were able to purchase additional land from the slave owners. That's how the people in this area became landowners. And, of course, there were some who had reservations about having any interference whatsoever when the civil rights movement came to the area. They were in their comfortable zones, perhaps, and having the civil rights workers come down to the community would only interfere with their . . . comfortable zone. Therefore, they felt that it was not necessary to make any changes. It's like they were living in their own little world there.

One of the persons who *was* very interested, a man that I always admired, was Mr. Henry Reaves. He was a landowner, but he didn't hesitate to step forward to do what is necessary to bring about a change. Mr. Reaves was a father figure to myself and a lot of the other young men in the community. And he was advising us of the things to expect and what was going on. I recall one time, I think I was about thirteen years of age, he had invited me to go with him to Pontotoc, Mississippi. There was a meeting going on down there and I went with him. He said, "You guys are too young to know what's going on. But you know black people have been suppressed for a long time, and black people have been denied certain rights." And he said, "You know, change is going to come, but it takes people to step forward. I don't have any fear of it, although it might cost a little bit. Sometimes it costs money. Sometimes it costs lives." And then he said, "But the biggest thing it costs right now is just time, and sacrifice. That's why I am busy doing what I'm doing." And he had a brother named Charlie Reaves who was very instrumental in that, as well.

Having been so young, with limited knowledge of what's happening in the world, it didn't all seem to paint a picture, at the time. But as time came and went, I began to gather up the pieces and see how it really painted a very clear picture as to where we came from, where we were, and where we were headed to. You know, all that came together. Even as I advanced in age and gained more knowledge of what life was like elsewhere—that is, in other countries and especially in the United States as a whole—and I saw, then, that the South must be a place that people like to run from because of the conditions there. And they was right. It was not a future.

There was a gentleman in the community named Ernest Matthews. He was kind of like Henry Reaves. He was a landowner in the Mount Zion community. And before school session had opened for the fall 1965, he was coming through the community, just trying to get some of what he called "students that would be interested in going up to the Ashland white school to begin the process of integration." I was in tenth grade, so he asked me, along with some other students in the community. And I said yeah, I would. It was an adventure to me. You know, I had always kept an open mind to experiment with something different, something new. And to me, that was just an avenue to venture out, not knowing what I would be confronted with at the time. But I think I was prepared to accept whatever it was that awaited me. In this case, there was a lot of criticism, a lot of prejudice in that school system. But at the time when

Mr. Ernest Matthews had confronted me about that, he said, "Well, we gotta have somebody to do this, and I think you'd be a good person to take a lead role in that." So I did it, you know? I made the best of it.

◆ ◆ ◆

Whenever something new came, it would go to the Ashland School, where the whites were. They would get them first, and then when they passed the old books, desks, and chairs on down to the black school, you know. They didn't throw anything away. It wasn't good enough for them, but yet it was too good to throw away. So why not pass it on to those people at the other schools.

Students in the school system there, they would provoke fights in the classroom. Like, "Nigger, why are you here? Don't you have your own school? Why don't you go back to your school?" And it seems if though the teacher knew that her students was going to do that. Each day she would make it a point, every day after the bell rang, when the session started, to leave her classroom for as much as three to five minutes. To give the kids the chance to really attack the blacks. And that was what happened. So I decided that I had had enough. Rather than stay seated, I decided to get up and defend myself, and I did. I think she was posted at the door to hear the commotion, waiting for the opportunity to come in at a time I was out of my seat, which she did. I got up out my seat and physically attacked a student. I had been hit and beaten with books and everything else, you know, and that was enough. But when the teacher come in, I was out of my seat, so she took me to the principal's office and explained to him what happened. I was denied the opportunity to explain to the principal what went on. It's like he heard her side of it, and that was it. And he said, "One more time, you're out of this school."

So the next week, the same thing happened. And it did happen, again, so he expelled me from school. I was there just for a short period of time, probably about two months. They had a policy—if you come from one school in the county and go to Ashland High, you cannot go back. So, therefore, you are out of school. You're a dropout. And that's the way they had it set up. They wanted me to drop out. So rather than dropping out, I went to Tippah County to finish high school. My father had gone up there and talked, but it didn't do any good. They said, "Well, it's the policy, the school policy." I think it was something that they just kind of drafted up because they anticipated there would be a lot of dropouts. And, and of course, you know, there were some who dropped out. There were some who did like myself, went elsewhere to finish school. But nevertheless I think that through all of that, there was something very victorious that came about. It's that persistence paid off with the students who were in the school system that year. And I think we kind of paved the way for the others who came there after us.

I think it had a very positive impact on me. It helped me when I became a young adult and moved to other areas. Especially in my military days, it helped cope with a lot of unnecessary type of circumstances. The things that I hear, negative remarks or name-calling, and certain circumstances where they do things to insult you, it helped me to brace myself for those type of things later in life. And even today, when I hear something, especially name-calling, it doesn't bother me. I think my background prepared me for that. And then I can, I think, pass that on or teach it to someone else now.

**Interviewer:** *Were there any white students or white teachers, in your two months at Ashland, that were at all friendly or helpful?*

Yeah, there were some there who were . . . who tried, by all means. Yeah, I remember one young man that offered me a pencil. He thought I didn't have a pencil. He wanted to let me have his pencil. There were those who were supportive. There were. And you will find, everywhere you go, even if there was only ten people, you would find two good people out of those ten who would seem to always be supportive of that which is right.

◆ ◆ ◆

I was working in Holly Springs as a clerk. So I went on to several areas for me to learn about postal management, postal supervision. I took corresponding courses. I already had an associate's degree at the time. So I took all their courses and it was approved. Then I applied to become an OIC,[3] and I did. There was no OIC in Ashland, so I got that area. And when I worked in Ashland for that period of time, you know, people came in and looked, and just . . . *looked*. It's like disapproval, you know, with that type of expression on their face. "How did you get up in here?" That was the question ringing from just about every other person came in the post office. "How did you get up in here?" How can somebody you try to suppress all your life come back to be over you in a position that a lot of whites wanted?

That was the first exposure I had in management. And after that I kept applying and applying. And finally I landed my first postmaster job way down in an area near Vicksburg. And after that I proved myself and I kept on advancing. I went to a post office in Bolivar, Tennessee, and I think I must've been the only black that would work there. And, there's a lady came in the post office to purchase a stamp. And there was a white, young lady that worked

Jimmie Cathey at his home after our conversation. Courtesy of John Lyons.

there. And so she came . . . I was still at the front. And she just came out, and just kept looking around, looking around, as if she was looking for something or someone. I said, "Ma'am, may I help you?" She said, "Uh, I was looking for Sherri." I said, "Well, she's not here. Is there anything I can help with?" "Well, I came to buy a stamp." I said, "Well, I'll sell you one." "I guess I'll just have to wait till Sherri come back." I said, "Ma'am, now, you have a choice. You either purchase a stamp from me, or you can go to Jackson, Tennessee, which is the next closest post office, which is sixty miles." She said, "Well, thank you." She walked out of the post office. [Laughs.] She would not purchase a stamp from me.

I received several postmaster positions. Choctaw County, which is in north central Mississippi. There, I was confronted by some . . . they call themselves "rednecks" or whatever. I was the only person in there of color. The community was a majority white. The workforce was white. Of course, I was met with a lot of resentment, and the administrators, principals, the bankers, and everybody else there, totally against it. One lady came forward and told me, "The peoples in this community have not accepted you." They had one of their local friends who was a highway patrolman followed me every time I went home. My employees saw fit that they would leave their work and would go outside and congregate beyond their five-minute break. So when I had a little talk with them, that was the one day the patrolman gave me a ticket. One hundred sixty dollars.

I stayed there until the time came when I was trying to get back to this area to help out with my father, who had become very ill. So I downgraded from a large office to a small office up in Michigan City [Benton County]. Well, Michigan City was different. It was a laidback community of a few people, a small office. Well, they did an article in the paper. They did all they can to disguise my name. They would not come forward with the correct name.

My days in high school prepared me for all this. So this had been an ongoing thing for a long time, so I think I had built up an immune system. And I just kind of anticipated that these things will happen and so it didn't bother me.

◆ ◆ ◆

If I had to do it all over again, I think that I would have used better judgment on my own behavior. I think I would have reacted with a sense of humor when those kids was provoking me. And I think, if I had to do it again, I wouldn't show any weakness whatsoever. You use a little bit of psychology on people, and when you see you can't get next to them, you just back off. You leave them alone. And I think I would have done something like that. But see, when they find your weakest area, that's what they continue to work and dwell on, to provoke it, you know. Expressing any sign weakness, once you show that, you just already surrendered yourself.

Life in the South is whatever you make out of it, you know. If you choose to let people hold you down, then I think you'll be held down. But if you choose to surface beyond the obstacles, that is to be able to find the ways to get around it, you can. If you look for a way of doing something, you'll find a way.

# Patrick Washington

## Born 1975

Interviewed August 2010, Ashland, Mississippi, by Aviva Futorian, Roy DeBerry, and John Lyons

*The fifth generation of educators in his family, Dr. Washington taught in the Memphis School System and was eventually named principal at age twenty-seven, the youngest principal in the district. After observing the lack of leadership in the Benton County School District, he decided to move back home and run for superintendent. Running as a young progressive, he was elected the first black superintendent of Benton County Schools in 2008. He was met with immediate opposition by the school board, who voted to decrease his salary by almost 30 percent. When he refused to grant jobs to people connected to the previous superintendent, more opposition arose, and he was defeated after one term by Jack Gaad, a white state representative from the southern part of the county. Dr. Washington sat down with us in his office halfway through his first term in 2010. At the time, the superintendent's office was located in the Benton County Courthouse, which was built by enslaved people.*

◆ ◆ ◆

I was born in Union County because, of course, there's no hospital in Benton County. I'm a native Benton Countian. My wife and I both graduated from Ashland High School, class of '93. My entire schooling was here. My great-grandfather worked at the cotton gin in Hudsonville. I was told that someone taught him to read. And after work he would sit around and teach some of his fellow laborers how to read. My mom was an educator with Benton County Schools for about thirty-two years. I have three siblings that have worked in the school system, so I guess teaching is kind of in our blood.

**Interviewer:** *What made you decide you wanted to be school superintendent in Benton County?*

I can't say honestly that I wanted to be superintendent. But I thought it was kind of ironic. Two particular weekends I was shopping and there were two parents that come to me. They were asking me questions about the services that their children were receiving in special education. And both parents ended the conversation by asking me, would I consider coming home to run for superintendent?

I guess their questions just kind of continued to haunt me a little bit. You know, my parents live here, I have a lot of family that live here. I decided to call my predecessor at the time and ask him if I could have a meeting with him. I really didn't know what I was going to say. I just wanted to meet him and just kind of see what his thoughts were on where he thought the school district was headed. And in this particular office, I met him, and he thought I wanted a job.

So he began to tell me that there was no positions open. And I asked him, "What was the mission and the vision of Benton County Schools?" And he couldn't give me an answer. So at that point I was like, "This school district's just kind of existing. It's just kind of floating along and wherever it lands or however the students perform is okay." I shared those thoughts and his response, or lack of response, with my wife, and I counseled with a couple of superintendents in the area. And, of course, prayed over it, and decided to get into the race.

Being black from Mississippi or the from the South in general, you have to get used to or accustomed to being treated differently. I knew early on that Mississippi had this stigma attached to it that I would somehow have to try to overcome. And I engaged in some conversations with individuals during the campaign that were a little bit different.

The challenges have been different. I really didn't have I guess a sound knowledge of the politics in Benton County. And I wasn't, even though I was a native son, I wasn't part of the inner circle of the politics. And so initially, even though the school district was identified as a district that was failing, there were a lot of decisions I felt like I needed to make. But I was just completely denied. The first item on the agenda was to lower the superintendent's salary, which I can certainly understand that. But the way in which it happened, I wasn't a part of that conversation. At the time, even though we're the second poorest county in the state, we had one of the highest paid superintendents. And it was—there was not a lot of emphasis placed on what going to be the new action plan and try to correct some of these things. It was just, "We need to control this guy. We need to set his salary and let him know who's in charge."

Benton County courthouse, former superintendent offices. Courtesy of John Lyons.

Patrick Washington (second from left) in the Hill Country Project office. Courtesy of Aviva Futorian.

And that's been difficult because the superintendent can't really be effective if he doesn't have the political support.

I've grown. I'm choosing my battles more wisely. I'm trying to keep the emphasis on what we need to do to really make schools better for students. And it's obvious when you go into our schools, we are a segregated school district, we all know that. And those are conversations that I'm comfortable having. A lot of people feel like it's political suicide to mention some of those things, like what are we going to do to bring more diversity to our schools? But the economy in Benton County and the school system are interrelated. If you don't improve the schools, we don't have to worry about people bringing businesses here.

I didn't come in here to put something else on my resume. I mean, this is home. I have a great deal of pride here. I want—I believe that we can be a school district that is known for excellence. We're no longer a failing district, we're successful. We had the highest dropout rate in northeast Mississippi, 31.5 percent. We decreased that in one year to 19.5 percent. Is it where we want to be? No, but it is progress. So that means what we're doing is working. You know, you may not like me, but you can look at the work and realize that something is working.

Our generation, after the civil rights movement, there was this false sense of: "We made it." You know, you removed the "white only," the "black only" signs. Now, without the signs, what do we march for? Well, we march for equity in public education. We know that, historically, the schools that were in the white communities did get better teachers and did get more resources. And we've seen that on some level here. And many of the students who attend Benton County Schools, their parents were my classmates. And they are adamant about not just making sure we have quality teachers, but just trying to bring more resources. We don't have a football team[4] in the entire county. They want to see things like that happen.

I think this generation wants to know, "How do we really make sure we have a voice?" And I think there's something else. I believe that my being elected has shown that we do have a voice. Sixty-one percent of the voting constituency is white and 36 percent black. We have a voice. It's not just about a color, but it's about doing what's right and making sure you use your right to vote. They realize now that every election counts for something.

## Chapter 7

# LOOKING BACK, LOOKING AHEAD

*The focus of* Voices from the Mississippi Hill Country *has been the role that some black people played in the life of Benton County before, during, and after the civil rights movement. At its core, the movement was about changing hearts and expanding minds. Our final two interviewees, though separated in age by decades, explore those themes while reflecting on the past and anticipating a better future.*

# Trevell Perdue

## Born 1996

Interviewed March 2018, via phone by John Lyons

*A sophomore at Rust College, Trevell is a poet, singer, and musician who was one of the students involved in oral history projects facilitated by the Hill Country Project, "My Space, My Story" and "Civil Rights, It's Happening Now." Like the vast majority of black students today, he began school at Ashland. When he grew restless there, he transferred to Hickory Flat, the white school, something he did to "try to form myself as a person." The great-grandson of Nelma and Albert Tipler, he spoke with us by phone in between classes at Rust.*

◆ ◆ ◆

When I first started school, I went to Ashland Elementary. It was predominantly black. We had a couple of white kids, six or seven. The white kids that we did have, obviously, it was their choice to stay at Ashland, so out of those people that attended, we didn't have a problem. It was like they were one of us. They didn't even want to be left out. You wouldn't find them sitting in the corner or anything. They'd be right there in the group with us having fun.

I made it to seventh grade in Ashland before I transferred to Hickory Flat. I had gotten tired of Ashland. One of my best friends, he attended Hickory Flat at the time, so, of course, that made me want to go. Maybe this was better for me, because I was just looking for something new and really try to form myself as a person. Like go to my next level, pay attention more in class. I was trying to be more open, I guess. I knew how it felt to grow up with my culture, or the people that look like me, I had to experience something new and I knew it.

I expected the racial aspect, to go in there and be prejudged. I knew people would look at me different. I knew I just couldn't go in doing what I wanted. I had to think about what I was doing down there.

Some of the teachers, they love you, offer the best support. Whatever they can help you with, it was there. They let you know you have somebody there that was looking out for you. But then you have some of those teachers who just view you as a goofball. They didn't treat you with the same love or give you the opportunity of a relationship that they would everybody else. Although they were good people, because they didn't spit in my face—you understand me? At least I could turn around, and you may still spit behind me, but I couldn't see you.

At home or at Ashland, I was just "Trevell." I can take being picked on by the people who look like me, but when I went to Hickory Flat, people would call you names. For the students there, I was just this weird, funny, black kid. That's how they treated me. When I went to compare Ashland and Hickory Flat . . . when I went to Hickory Flat, I got in more trouble.

When I got down there, I had this altercation with this white kid on a bus. We were on the bus on our way home, and it was this white guy, I knew him. One day we were on the bus, me and my friend, joking around. And this guy saw us. And he joined in on us, like playing around. And he's calling me the "B" word. I was on the bus, and I and my friend was like, "Oh. You going to let him call you this?" This was what was going on, so we got into an altercation. I bruised him, I guess, and he pressed charges on me. I got this simple assault charge. He was saying that I was a bully. I've never been known to be a bully. That's what made me leave Hickory Flat. I ended up going to alternative school, which was held in Ashland, so I said, "I'm coming back to Ashland."

I had come to the realization of what things were. It was like, "Hey, this is Ashland, and all of the black people have been going here and then there's Hickory Flat." My granddad, I think he attended Ashland. His name is Jimmy Noren. I think he attended the school around when all of the whites were leaving.

Today, black people, we can interact with the opposite race, and naturally we just show respect. Let's say we go out, we're walking in the store or something like that, we may not acknowledge every person we see, but we're going to smile. You have the people who are like us, who are open to *not* seeing color.

But I still, to this day, can go over to Shortstop [a convenience store across from the dorms at Rust] and get asked by one of the white workers, "What you want?" and I can feel offended in a way. I understand you've got this job, or whatever, I don't know what's been going on before, but I'm showing you respect, I want that same respect. I shouldn't be feeling tension while I'm trying to shop with your store. I'm not comfortable with it.

Trevell Perdue at the Mississippi Department of Archives
and History performance. Courtesy of John Lyons.

**Interviewer:** *What frightens you?*

Honestly? Failing. Not becoming anything. I attend Rust College, majoring in
mass communications. When I first came here, I wanted to major in business
and then I wanted to own something or to do something. But I had this talent.
I could sing, and I could write poems. So I came to Rust. I came for my poetry.
I feel like I'm going to impress the world in some sort of way, either with music
or poetry, honestly.

    In some areas, our generation is well aware of what was going on with civil
rights. I owe it to those people, because without them we wouldn't even have
this chance to attend school, to write poetry. Black people weren't even allowed
to educate themselves. If they were caught reading, they would be punished
for reading, trying to learn. Yes, we owe it to them. They had a vision that we
weren't slaves. They had a vision that we could vote. They had a vision that we

were equal. With this vision, if you're fighting for us and you pave the way, I can put up a little bit of fight, too. It's not that hard anymore, so I should be able to throw a couple of punches. I'm doing it by whatever I write.

Too many people have dreamed, and too many people have died. Knowing the things that I do know about history, I just have to be somebody. I have to be somebody. All I want to do is touch the world, make a difference.

# Lillie Ree Duffie

## Born 1948

Interviewed November 2012, Chicago, Illinois, by Aviva Futorian and John Lyons

*The ninth of fourteen children, Ms. Duffie desegregated Ashland High School at the age of sixteen. When we sat down in her home on the south side of Chicago, it was clear she has a vivid memory of her experiences. It's also clear that she has profound empathy for the white students she attended school with, many of whom tormented her during her time there: "I never held anything against them. They were children. They were trying to find a way, just like I was."*

◆  ◆  ◆

My father[1] bought one hundred acres, and we were farmers. That was his profession. I remember unfairness to my father and my family. My dad would pick cotton on our farm and then he would take the cotton to the gin. We would get the seed and we would sell the cotton and the seeds. He didn't get much for the stuff at all. He would have to go and borrow money to grow crops. I remember this particular time, he didn't have enough money to buy his seeds. And this merchant charged him . . . God, I don't know how much, but quite a bit. And that bill seemed never to get paid and there was always more added to the bill, all the time. Until my dad just had to put us to work onto another farm to help pay this particular person out.

If we would go to the store, we always was waited on last if there were white people in the store. If we were there first, we would be put in the back of the line. When they received money from us, when we finally get to the counter, it was snatched from our hands. They would never touch our hands because you're black, you know? We couldn't drink from the same water fountain, and they had signs up saying, "colored only," "whites only." And we knew because our parents taught us, "No, no. Don't drink from the white fountain," because we don't know what could happen to you, so we made sure we drink from the colored only fountain.

My mom took sick one time, she had arthritis so bad and her blood pressure was sky high. My dad had to take her to the doctor's office in the city of Holly Springs, and there was "colored only" and "white only" waiting rooms, so when my dad took her in the colored waiting room, by the time they finished covering all the white patients, this doctor got ready to call my mother in. And then another white woman walked in and they said, "Oh no. Never mind." And they called this white lady's name. She saw that my mom was crying, she was aching so badly. And this white lady said, "Oh no. Take her, take her." I thought that was kind of her, and then the doctors saw my mom. But that's what it was.

You know, we never asked why because it was always like that. They told us what we already had figured out and knew—that we just didn't mix. We saw what was happening, It was all around us. We knew that this is a way of life.

◆　◆　◆

My memories of civil rights . . . I have to go back to Little Rock, Arkansas.[2] We watched that on our little TV monitor in the house, and I remember my mom said to us, "You know in a couple of years this is going to be happening here." I remember my stomach just like . . . got queasy. After watching what happened in Little Rock and how the hatred was so prevalent there, I knew out in Mississippi it probably wouldn't be any better. Maybe worse. I was *petrified*. And a couple of years later, sure enough. It wasn't pleasant, those memories, but I knew that there was something that I was called to do.

What made me want to go Ashland to be part of integration is because I knew there was something more than what I was getting. I knew that there was going to be a future for me, and I needed to do something more. I knew that it was going to be difficult, but I knew also that I wasn't a quitter. There was this strong urge in me that was driving me to do this. I had to go, not only for myself, but to help make a pathway for others. I am the ninth child of fourteen, and there were quite a few siblings behind me that needed to do better.

I talked to my parents about integrating, and my mom said, "Are you sure that's what you want to do?" "Yes, I think so." She said, "Okay, go for it." My dad would say, "If your mom says it's okay, do it. But you know, it's not going to be easy." What I saw in Little Rock, I knew it wasn't going to be easy.

I remember the first day of school, that bus pulling up. I had been standing there with my younger brothers, one on each side of me and squeezing their hands. Getting on that bus . . . oh my God, everybody got quiet. We stepped on the bus, looking for somewhere to sit. I held tightly to my little brother's hand. We went to the back because those were the seats that were available. It was not pretty at all. Being called every name you can imagine. The driver would not allow you to get on the bus and sit down; he just pressed onto the accelerator and you'd fall. I was nervous, my baby brother was nervous, you know? I remember putting my arm around him and holding him a little closer . . . he just held onto me. But that wasn't the point. There was a bigger picture than that. That's what I had to keep in my mind. And I told my brother, "You know, you're not going there for any other reason but to get an education. That's why I am with you."

We finally made it to the school, and all those parents out there, all lined on the sidewalk to try to prevent us from even going to school. We weren't there for any other reason than to help better ourselves. To get an education. And you could cut the hate with a knife. I couldn't understand that. And then there was some people that were there to help make a path, so that we could go through. I was separated from my brother because he was in first grade. And I kept wondering, "What is happening with him?"

◆ ◆ ◆

After integration, there would be a grove of cars right before the sun went down. Klansmen. They would be blowing their horns, coming down from Hudsonville Road. I remember cars stopping where we lived, and they put a cross up there. Set it on fire. They were all white, hooded, with eyes cut out. And yes, I remember my dad would get his gun and go out the back kitchen door because he wanted to protect us, you know? I remember hearing voices from outside saying, "Nigger, nigger!" And we were scared, so my mom made us lay flat on the floor. Flat. I was scared, but I had faith in my dad. He was going to take care of us. But I could see fear in my dad's face. My dad would drive us to the school bus stop and he would put his rifle in the back of his car. I could see how he would be looking around, but he never once, out of all that happened, he never *once* told us to quit. We kept going because Dad was there to protect us.

My worst memory: I was changing class from library and going down to economics. They were in two different buildings. There was a group of white girls that all gathered together. And they stood on the sidewalk and said, "Go around, nigger!" Well, I had a bumpy ride that morning and I really didn't feel like getting off the sidewalk. I stood back and said, "No, you move!" You know, I knew better than that, because we were taught nonviolence, okay? Well this just was not one of my better mornings. I said, "No you move. I am on the sidewalk and I am going through," and then one girl pushed me, knocked me off the sidewalk. I politely put my books down, and I pushed back. And then she yelled, she's right in the center of all the girls, "Don't push me, nigger! You pushed me!" Well, I yelled back. "You pushed me first, girl!" and when I said, "girl," oh, she flipped! So a teacher saw us and saw that I didn't back down and took us both to the office. She was telling the principal, "This nigger girl pushed me," and I said, "No this honky girl pushed me," very loud. The principal told us, "If the two of you don't stop, I'm going to suspend both of you, okay?" Gave us good talking too. I got my books and headed back to home economics, and the remaining children that was on the sidewalk parted the way, let me through.

I think it was a learning process. Someone had to teach you to hate in order for you to be that way. So I felt kind of sorry for them, in a way, because it had to be difficult to think that. The worst things happened with the children that was from poor white families. These really poor kids, they would be the ones sitting in the middle seats of the bus, calling us names and sticking their feet out. Sayin', "Go to the back." I caught on to that right away. So, in the lunchroom if I needed to sit someplace, I would find where the more prominent kids were sitting. And even if I sat at the end, they wouldn't get up and move. They stayed there. But if I sat at the end of a table with these poor kids, oh gosh. They would *run*. They didn't wanted be identified as being around a black person. Because then the prominent kids won't have anything to do with them. I understood their pain, too. I really did. Honestly, it's a painful thing to be that way. That you have to always watch who you speak to and who you'd be around.

The kids I went to school with, that I integrated into, it wasn't easy for them either. I shed tears, mostly for the ones that were ignorant. If they had come to Old Salem, we wouldn't have done that to them. But they didn't know any better. I think that whole experience not only helped us, but helped them. The girl on the sidewalk, I think what she got out of integration was a knowledge that every black person is not going to just be pushed around. I am pretty sure she realized that, in her future, she'll be running up against people like that little black girl she ran up against on the sidewalk. There is more than just one race of people in the world, and you have to deal with all sort of people in order to make it.

# Acknowledgments

*Voices from the Mississippi Hill Country* was over two decades in the making. To complete such a task would not have been possible without the help, guidance, encouragement, and financial support of many people.

First and foremost, we offer our deepest thanks to the scores of interviewees with whom we spoke. Over one hundred residents of Benton County made time and opened their offices, churches, and homes to us. We are also grateful to the interviewees who introduced us to others who would eventually be included in this volume.

We also thank Gloria Clark, a SNCC volunteer in neighboring Tippah County, for the inspiration to undertake this project; Pat Buckley, for transcribing interviews; Matt Renuad of Jenner & Block for assistance with establishing our 501(c)3; Frank Cieciorka, for the use of an incredible photography collection; the Mississippi Humanities Council; the Mississippi Department of Archives and History; the Kellogg Foundation; Sheldon Baskin; and Wilbur Colom (who also participated in the earliest interviews), for financial support. We also wish to thank Hattie Gordon, Sarah Richard, Sonny Reaves, Charlie Walls, Bill Renick, Lisa Lynch, Elena Lewis, Rubye DeBerry, Jackie Rivet-River, Jessica Lyons, Patty Albrecht Glosik, Charles Tucker, Susan Glisson and the William Winter Institute, the University of Mississippi, Andre DeBerry, Alysia Steele, Ralph Eubanks, Clarence Hunter, Anne Sapps, the Benton County Historical Society, the Benton County Library, Columbia College Chicago, Jeff Spitz, Michael Weaver and Sencha Systems, Dr. Jeanne Middelston-Hairston, Mount Zion CME Church, Jerry Watson and Rust College, and countless others.

# Editors' Note

The beginning of our editorial team was formed in 1964 during what was called Freedom Summer, when Aviva Futorian—a young, white high school teacher from the northern suburbs of Chicago—volunteered to travel to Mississippi to work with the Student Nonviolent Coordinating Committee. When she began working in Benton County, she met a sixteen-year-old civil rights activist from Holly Springs named Roy DeBerry. That autumn, SNCC assigned Aviva to work as an "organizer" in Benton County. In addition to working with the Citizens Club she taught a college prep class there. Roy was in her class, and a friendship was cemented.

Thirty years later, in 1994, the idea for this project was born at a Freedom Summer reunion, attended by both Roy and Aviva. As old friends were reacquainted, talk eventually turned to what comes next and a common theme was discovered. Young people in the South, the North, black and white, had a woeful lack of understanding of the civil rights movement. Children and grandchildren had little or no idea, the roles their forebears played in the shaping of American history. Aviva and Roy, together with fellow SNCC volunteer Gloria Clark (who had worked in neighboring Tippah County), decided to start capturing stories of the movement in their respective counties. With a basic video camera and a list of questions, the team began visiting local people they worked with in the 1960s and capturing those conversations on camera. Over fifteen hours of interviews were produced and transcribed in 1994. Aviva and Roy spent many hours walking the track at Rust College hammering out their ideas for whom to interview and what to discuss in the interviews.

Nearly ten years after that reunion, another was held in north Mississippi in the summer of 2003. In advance of that meeting, Aviva (now living in Chicago) enlisted the help of a local filmmaker she knew, John Lyons. He looked at the original 1994 footage and from it created a film called *My Mind Stayed on Freedom* to be screened at the reunion, which he attended.

In addition, John began filming the interviews, capturing video and audio at a higher quality than before, and Roy and Aviva continued to record the stories of Benton Countians. The trip in the summer of 2003 produced several more oral history interviews. It prompted another visit, with more interviews in early 2004, then another, and another. In 2007, Aviva reached out to her longtime friend, Stephen Klein, a writer, consultant, and expert in economic development with strong ties to the civil rights movement. Shortly thereafter, a 501(c)(3) status was sought and granted, office space was purchased, and the Hill Country Project was born. Roy DeBerry was named the organization's executive director. In addition to capturing oral histories of Benton County's residents, the new organization's mission included supporting the county's education system. The intent was to reach young people through mentoring programs, college and career guidance, and instruction on capturing and editing oral history.

Almost twenty-five years after the meeting in Jackson, the Hill Country Project has captured over one hundred oral history interviews spanning more than a century of history, the results of which constitute this volume.

The project continues to support the county's educational system and mentor its students.

It is worth mentioning a few words about the interviews themselves and how they were conducted. The earliest conversations were recorded in 1995 and 2003, and were exclusively with people we had an existing relationship with. As the project became larger, we began reaching out to others Aviva and Roy had worked with in the 1960s, and then began meeting other Benton Countians whose contributions we felt were important. Sometimes they were people we'd heard of but hadn't met, while other times people were recommended to us by those we had already interviewed. Almost everyone we spoke to invited us into their homes.

Three of us are white—Aviva, John, and Stephen—and Roy is black. By and large, the decision of who would be present at each interview was based on availability rather than strategy. The exception to this was the chapter on white reactions (the only white participants in *Voices from the Mississippi Hill Country*) when we felt a more open conversation would be facilitated without the presence of Roy. Sometimes interviews with black participants were conducted by only white interviewers, but usually these were conducted with people with whom we had prior relationships. While not an exact science, we utilized our best judgement. In certain instances, mutual friends or family of the participant were present during the interview to facilitate introductions and in some cases, help jog memories. A note is made in the introduction as to who was present during the interview.

Interviews lasted from forty-five minutes to close to three hours, with some participants being interviewed more than once. Almost all interviews were videotaped, and the few that weren't were recorded by audio. We transcribed the entirety of each interview through a combination of our own work, volunteers, and professional services, and then checked each transcript for accuracy against the recording. Each interview we included in *Voices from the Mississippi Hill Country* was then edited for length and clarity. That said, we made every attempt to preserve the speaking and grammatical style of the participant, along with local expressions and idioms.

# Appendix I: Early Black Registered Voters

This is a list of black people who registered to vote in Benton County between 1902 and 1938 (some registrations are crossed out for failure to pay poll tax). It was copied from an old voter registration book in the circuit clerk's office.

### Canaan Precinct District 1: (8 blacks registered)

Ben Walls, Sam Bostick, EPJ Brown, John Smith, Walter Parham, JFW Hoyle, Arthur Bostick, WL Spencer. No black registrants after 1931.

### Maxey's Store District 4: (5)

JW Davis, LA Gholson, Robert Stewart, Arthur Bostick, Sam Bostick. No black registrants before 1919 or after 1931.

### Hamilton Precinct District 1: no black voter registrants

### Michigan City Precinct District 2: (47)

Wilson Golson, WJ Hubbard, Watt Stornes, Oliver Maxey, John Rutherford, Freelin Brown, Henry Jackson, Lee Williamson, SM Williamson, Jessie Coley, Amos Blackwell, Will Bosley, Robert Epps, Jessie Pointer, Henry Shelton, Jim Thompson, Earnest Epps, Perry Kilgore, Clarance Wyatt, Jim Watkins, Jack Spencer, Robert S. Williams, Frank Grahan, David Bramlett, Clarence Williams, EW Watkins, Hardy Strickland, RB Williams, Sam Williams, Audrey Terry, John Moore, Lawson Turner, Edd Pointer, JL Hicks, JW Hicks, WM Williamson, Ella White (female!), RA Littleton, Laura Jackson (female!), George Epps, Syrus Perry, Lee Jimerson, Clabon Jackson, Alex Greer, Marvin Shelton, CR Wyatt, Henry Davis

### Lamar Precinct District 2: (26)

Henry Watson, MC Evans, EC Baird, Elex Seay, JK Evans, Preston Evans, ES Baird, Claibron Evans, James Bean Sr., Dick Gholston, AM Washington, John Bell, Ned Greene, AT Jeffries, Jessie Avant, Jim Young, Tom McKennie, Laurence Cleaver, Lewis Brown, George Harris, Edd Cleaver, Baker Humpherys, Will Ray, Henry Rhyneheart, RL Evans, Salon Peterson. No black registrants after 1927.

### Ashland Precinct District 3: (23)

NH Williamson, Sol Rutherford, Charlie Baird, AG Gibson, Tom Mathis, JW Crawford, GW Hamer, JE Everett, Sam Wright, MP Price, Willie Mitchell, Nathan Luellen, JW Mason, Henry Beck, John Richard, Frank Baird, Major Baird, BV Elliott, Robert Cole, Arthur Hodges, James Elliott, Harvey Mathews, Charlie Littleton. No black registrants after 1919.

Registration did not appear to be limited to black landowners, as long as the registrant could pay the poll tax. Many of the above registrants appear to list other people as their employers (i.e., on whose land they farmed). It was said if a white man "vouched" for a black man, he was allowed to register.

# Appendix 2: Black Landownership in Benton County

Coeditor Aviva Futorian obtained the following information from the 1870 Census in addition to interviewing black Benton Countians during her time there as a volunteer in the 1960s.

The 1870 census of Tippah County-Salem Post office area (subsequently Benton County) lists the first three black landowners as M. Boatner, Wash Collier, Aaron Cooper.

The area known as Little Egypt at some point had a lot of black landowners. Nan Gibson, John Farese's housekeeper, lived there, as did (or do) the Wilsons, Hudsons, Jacksons. The north end of Snow Lake Shores was all black-owned; it is now a white-owned resort area.

Dick Robertson, born in 1833, the son of a white man and an enslaved woman, acquired over three thousand acres of land in Benton (at the time Tippah) County. He made money by storing cotton with a white half brother during the Civil War and then selling it at inflated prices after the war. He died in 1901. We are not sure if mismanagement by his sons or white theft depleted the estate. A good deal of his land ended up in the hands of the Double O Ranch, north of Highway 72 above Highway 5.

Part of the Double O Ranch was called Berry Hill Place and belonged to Harry MacAmee, a black man who owned land and had a successful business. He was killed by a white man, and his land was appropriated by whites. His widow was still living in the 1960s.

Much of the area around Michigan City was owned by blacks, including Dick Robertson, after the Civil War until 1900. Ella Bailey was a large landowner. She ran a restaurant in Michigan City. She was run out of Mississippi.

Large white landowners such as Joe Hardaway and the McKenzies would sell off some of their land to blacks. Willingness to sell land might have had to do with the Depression.

Joe King may have been one of the earliest and largest black landowners in Benton County (this would have been the father of Joe King who put up land for Aviva Futorian's bail in 1965). So was Alfred Gipson, who had land near Good Hope (Little Egypt). Other early landowners were Sachs Pamm, Dick Robertson, Perry Hill, Doug Perry, Tom Mathis (Mathews), Landy Perry, Freelin Brown, Alford Hoyle, John Crawford, Len Brown, Mose Terry, Wheeler Mathews, W. C. Royston, A. T. Royston, Clea Rutherford, Robert Beard, Mel Price, Eugene Steward's father (Robert), and Levi Reaves (Henry Reaves's father). Will Ray, Earnestine Scott's great-grandfather, bought land from Isaac Peterson, who had bought it at some point.

A number of black people bought land in the early 1940s: Nelma Tipler's father, Sam White; Nelma's father-in-law, Miller Tipler; and Joe Bean, who bought as well as inherited land.

# Notes

## Introduction

1. According to the 2010 US Census.

2. In the area of what would become Benton County, there were cotton gins in Michigan City, Ashland, Lamar, Hopewell, Hickory Flat, as well as on private farms. Most of these towns had more than one gin. In addition to vast amounts of cultivated land, the area also had thousands of acres of forests. Lumber was therefore an important industry as well. Ashland alone had at least ten sawmills, one of which was owned by Mack Luellen, an African American. Marie Charles, *History of Benton County, Mississippi: The First 70 Years 1870–1940*, pp. 180–181.

3. Senator Revels is buried in Hill-Crest Cemetery in Holly Springs, fifteen miles from Benton County.

4. *Ashland Register*, October 30, 1879.

5. *Ashland Register*, August 7, 1879.

6. *Ashland Register*, November 6, 1879.

7. *Ashland Register* 1, no. 15 (September 25, 1979).

8. This approach was further cemented into law by the US Supreme Court ruling in 1896 of *Plessy v. Ferguson*, which established the concept of "separate but equal." So long as facilities and services for blacks and whites were "equal," racial segregation was legal.

9. One of the contributing factors to Benton's strong civil rights movement in the twentieth century was the significant amount of black landownership. See Appendix 2.

10. Reconstruction saw the establishment of Samuel's Chapel School, Sander's Chapel school, New Hope, Good Hope (one of the oldest), Berry's Chapel (later known as Sim's Chapel School), New Bethel, Mount Zion, Chapel Hill (later Shiloh), Center Hill, and Hamer School. As of 1899, records show forty-seven white schools and between twenty-six and thirty black schools in Benton County. Later, in the nineteenth and early twentieth centuries, black citizens established Mt. Mariah School, Harris Chapel, Gift Hill, the Lewellen School, Clemmer, Clayton Line School, Drivers, Meadows, Boothes Chapel, Meridian, Old Salem, Lane, New Salem, Mason, Green Spring (later Michigan City), Thompson, Palestine, and Royston Chapel School.

11. As late as 1960, only 4.2 percent of the state's black adults had held high school diplomas. *Census of the Population: 1960, Volume I, Characteristics of the Population: Part 26, Mississippi* (Government Printing Office, 1961), 26–118.

12. State Normal, Rust, and Mississippi Industrial (M.I.) Colleges, all in Holly Springs. By 1936, black teachers were drawing an annual salary of $484, whereas white teachers were paid $1,585. *Race and Schooling in the South, 1880–1950: An Economic History, Volume 2*, ed. Robert Margo (January 1990).

13. Fleeing Mississippi became characteristic of people whose family members were lynched.

14. *Southern Advocate*, July 6, 1933.

15. See appendix I.

16. Among the summer volunteers in Benton County that summer were Pete Cummings, Ralph Featherstone, Cleve Sellers, Bob Feinglass, Frank Cieciorka, Marjorie Merrill, Gloria Xifaras, Fern Gelford, Pam Parker, Michael Clurman, and Aviva Futorian.

17. Aviva Futorian is a coeditor of this book.

18. Clay Batts was a promising young leader who was very active in the movement; he died tragically in a drowning accident in Wisconsin in the summer of 1965. His brother Joe discusses him in chapter 6.

19. Black people in northern Mississippi first heard about the murder of Emmett Till from Pullman porters throwing copies of the *Chicago Defender* off the train.

20. The entire archive of the *Freedom Trains* is available digitally on hillcountryproject .org.

21. The MFPD was successful in seating a biracial delegation at the Chicago Democratic National Convention in 1968, including Henry Reaves.

22. *Benton County Freedom Train*, March 14, 1965.

23. The churches were Mount Zion, Hardaway, Sims, Palestine, and Greenwood.

24. *Benton County Freedom Train*, January 2, 1966.

25. They included Earl Price, Loyal Thompson, and Willie Lee "Bud" Beck. Eugene Steward, who worked in maintenance at the school, was also fired.

26. The women included Beulah Mae Ayers, Lorsie Jones (from Marshall County), Onie Lee Williams, Calburdia Tipler, Thelma Thompson, Delilah Evans, Mattie Smith, Betty Jordan, Mattie Mae Washington, Francis Thompson, and Allie Jane Beck. They wrote a report of the incident in the February 23, 1965, edition of *Freedom Train*.

27. Referring to Mark DeWolfe Howe's closing statement, one of the white residents was heard to say, "I don't care for those people, but that little guy sure could talk!"

28. Since very few blacks lived in that area, desegregation efforts did not affect the white student population there. In fact, white students from Ashland also began attending Hickory Flat, sometimes physically moving to be within the school's boundaries, sometimes using false addresses. This was so common that a bus stop at the northern border of Hickory Flat's district boundary was added.

### Chapter 1

1. A predecessor of the food stamp program for poor families. Occasionally, a corrupt landowner would collect the government commodities and sell it to the poor tenant farmers.

2. Her grandfather walked from Virginia to Mississippi at some point in the late 1860s following emancipation.

3. Mathis was the Benton County registrar, and would intimidate blacks attempting to register to vote. In addition, like most counties under Jim Crow, he would make blacks answer exceedingly difficult (and often irrelevant) constitutional questions, take literacy tests, and pay a poll tax in order to qualify to register.

4. Bob Moses was the field secretary for the Student Nonviolent Coordinating Committee (SNCC) and one of the main organizers of Freedom Summer in 1964, the project that brought hundreds of northern, white, and black volunteers to Mississippi to draw the nation's attention to the state's inequality.

5. Andrew Goodman, James Chaney, and Michael Schwerner were Freedom Summer volunteers who were working on voter registration when they disappeared near Philadelphia, Mississippi. Their burned-out car was found three days later, and after an intensive two-month search, their bodies were discovered in a dam.

6. The "split-session" school calendar meant that for black students, school began in the summer. It was let out in the spring and fall to allow those students to work in the fields. It was a schedule that prioritized manual labor over education.

7. Commonly referred to as a "poll tax," this practice was instituted as part of Jim Crow laws.

8. "Uncle Tom" was an epithet used against blacks who were exceedingly subservient to, or cooperative with, whites. It originated from Harriet Beecher Stowe's novel *Uncle Tom's Cabin*.

9. Smith Houey and Robert "Isey" Jones who were both lynched around 1933 in Ashland. They were lynched on Meridian Road in the northern part of the county, their bodies then brought to the courthouse in Ashland.

10. The Kudzu Café, a white owned segregated restaurant on the square in Ashland.

11. A daily newspaper in Memphis, Tennessee.

12. Owning land for blacks did allow a certain amount of independence. Many sharecroppers or renters would be threatened with eviction for involvement.

13. In addition to constitution tests, poll taxes, and other obstacles, the names of blacks who attempted to register were published in the local newspaper for three weeks, which led to further harassment, difficulty finding work and for sharecroppers or renters, threats of eviction.

14. A group of hundreds of students demonstrated in Jackson, Mississippi, for voting rights. The demonstrators were arrested and held in the state fairgrounds for nearly two weeks. Roy DeBerry, a coeditor of this book, was one of those arrested.

15. The MFDP was created by SNCC and other civil organizations in in 1964 to challenge the regular Mississippi Democratic Party because of its exclusion of blacks.

16. The actual quote in the magazine was: "Mr. Thompson hasn't shot his 12-gauge shotgun in *anger*. At least not yet." The shotgun Mr. Thompson owned was for hunting, and the photograph misled viewers into thinking he was a violent man.

17. Smith Houey and Robert "Isey" Jones, who were lynched in Benton County in the 1930s.

18. Mississippi Industrial College, a four-year private church-related college and high school for African American students, located in Holly Springs, Mississippi.

19. Fannie Lou Hamer, a famous activist from Sunflower County, Mississippi.

20. She was arrested for attending a basketball game at the black high school to which she was invited by the students in her college prep class.

21. W. B. Foster was the black principal at Old Salem, Benton County's black school. In 1965, a delegation of parents from the Citizens Club went to the county's superintendent of education and sought to remove Mr. Foster, who some black parents felt conceded too much to whites and didn't focus on providing a decent education for the black students.

22. The concept and organization for Freedom School was developed chiefly by Charlie Cobb, a member of SNCC.

23. Macedonia CME Church and Samuel's Chapel Baptist Church were both frequent locations for civil rights meetings.

24. The Federal Housing Administration.

25. Smith Houey and Robert "Isey" Jones, lynched together in Benton County in the 1930s.

## Chapter 2

1. Local white plantation owners.

2. The phrase "Reconstruction Days" was commonly used to refer to the post-Reconstruction period, a.k.a. Jim Crow.

3. Smith Houey and Robert "Isey" Jones, two victims of lynching in Benton County in the late 1930s.

4. A white school administrator for whom Spence sharecropped. He eventually hired Spence as a maintenance worker in the school system.

5. Nine black students enrolled in Central High School in Little Rock, Arkansas in 1957, one of the first major tests of the *Brown v. Board of Education* decision.

6. Henry Reaves.

7. Emmett Till was a young boy lynched in 1955 in Money, Mississippi, for allegedly whistling at a white woman. He was beaten, shot, and thrown into a river. When his body was discovered, his mother insisted on an open casket funeral. Images of his mutilated body were nationally published and became a catalyst for the civil rights movement.

8. Crystal Steward, their youngest child.

9. Naomi Reaves was the daughter of Henry and Ginevera Reaves. She passed away from leukemia at the age of twelve.

10. The "Freedom House," as it was called, was the office used by SNCC volunteers and the Citizens Club.

11. A pair of white brothers known for harassing black people, especially on the highways.

12. Nelma and Albert's young son.

13. The Freedom House was built on the Tiplers' land. From that office, the *Benton County Freedom Train* was printed and distributed clandestinely throughout the county, detailing activities of the movement.

14. Beulah Mae Ayers, the editor of the *Freedom Train*.

15. Dexter and Gaither's brother.

## Chapter 3

1. The names of honor roll students were published in the *Southern Advocate*, the local Benton County newspaper.

2. Old Salem, the black school that she left to attend Ashland.

3. Old Salem.

4. John Farese Sr., a local attorney, was a powerful figure in the community. He came to Mississippi from Massachusetts to attend school on an athletic scholarship at UM, married a southern girl, settled in Benton County, opened a law firm, and named his first child, John Booth Farese, after the assassin of Abraham Lincoln.

5. April 4, 1968, the day Martin Luther King Jr. was assassinated.

6. While some blacks voted during Reconstruction, the Reaves family were among the first blacks to vote in the modern era.

7. She is likely referring to Greenwood Church, where a lot of meetings were held.

8. Gray's Academy, a private school where most of the white students transferred to after integration began.

9. Landownership didn't necessarily preclude families from having to sharecrop. Several black families in Benton County owned land, but they did not make not enough cash to sustain them financially or nutritionally. In many cases, they were denied loans for housing, crop seeds, fertilizer, equipment, or other essentials so they were forced into sharecropping. They were considered as "land rich but cash poor."

10. Old Salem boycott.

11. The owner of the land. In the case of the Nelson family, it was Billy Carpenter.

12. Referring to the school boycott to get rid of the principal at Old Salem in early 1965.

## Chapter 4

1. After the first few years of integration of Ashland High School, white students began moving away to other counties, attending the private Gray Academy, or falsifying their address to attend Hickory Flat High School. By the mid-1970s, Ashland was an almost entirely black school.

2. He is apparently referring to the lynching of Smith Houey and Robert "Isey" Jones.

3. One of the Confederacy's most effective generals during the Civil War and a leader of the Ku Klux Klan afterward.

4. "Lightnin'" was the Rev. Henry Beard, a minister who was very active in the movement. His daughters, Ruth Ross and Peggy Simpson, were interviewed for this book.

5. The son of Walter Reaves, who was interviewed for this book

6. Freedom of Choice was a method by which black children could attend formerly all-white schools, but in staggered grades.

7. A term that was frequently used by white people who were opposed to integration.

8. Snow Lake Shores is a town in Benton County built around a lake. It's a separate municipality with roughly three hundred families, almost all white.

## Chapter 5

1. Mississippi Industrial College and High School in Holly Springs.

2. Likely, she meant the gym of Holly Springs High School.

3. Benton County Citizens Club Office.

4. John Farese, Benton County attorney.

5. Benton County registrar J. B. Mathis set up numerous roadblocks for blacks to vote over his twenty years in office.

## Chapter 6

1. During college Mr. Griffin opened a small convenience store in Lamar with money he had saved doing yard work.

2. The practice of "catching up" means the person who could pick faster would allow the slower picker to pull even.

3. Officer in charge, a step towards becoming the postmaster.

4. The school board held an executive session, with the sole purpose of reducing the salary of the newly elected superintendent. It was explained later by the board attorney to the people in the audience that the new superintendent had less experience than the outgoing superintendent. However, the board conceded that the new superintendent had a doctorate which would be equivalent to the experience. The motion was passed by the school board, and the superintendent's salary was reduced from $120,000 to $85,000. When Jack Gaad was elected, the original salary was restored.

## Chapter 7

1. Jake Nunnally was described by his mother-in-law Eldora Johnson as "the bravest black man I knew."

2. The integration of Central High School in Little Rock, Arkansas, took place in 1957, enforcing the *Brown v. Board of Education* Supreme Court decision from three years earlier. Because of the racist opposition from Governor Orval Faubus and major elements in the white community, President Dwight Eisenhower made a decision to send federal troops to provide security for the seven black students who integrated the school, which was enforcement of the *Brown v. Board of Education* Supreme Court decision in 1954.

# Bibliography

Arendt, Hannah. *Eichmann in Jerusalem: A Report on the Banality of Evil.* New York: Viking Press, 1963.

Arsenault, Raymond. *Freedom Riders: 1961 and the Struggle for Racial Justice.* New York: Oxford University Press, 2006.

Bettelheim, Bruno. *The Informed Heart: Autonomy in a Mass Age.* Glencoe, IL: Free Press of Glencoe, 1963.

Charles, Marie Smith. *History of Benton County, Mississippi: The First 70 Years, 1870–1940.* Benton County: Benton County Historical and Genealogical Society, 2009.

Clyde, Sharon. *Earth Eyes Destinations: Benton County, Mississippi.* n.d.

Dittmer, John. *Local People: The Struggle for Civil Rights in Mississippi.* Chicago: University of Illinois Press, 1994.

Eubanks, Ralph W. *Ever is a Long Time: A Journey into Mississippi's Dark Past.* New York: Basic Books, 2003.

Evers, Charles, and Andrew Szanton. *Have No Fear: A Black Man's Fight for Respect in America.* New York: A Robert L. Bernstein Book, 1997.

Hampton, Henry, and Steve Fayer. *Voices of Freedom: An Oral History of the Civil Rights Movement from 1950s through the 1980s.* New York: Bantam Books.

Horn, Teena F., Alan Huffman, and John Griffin Jones, eds. *Lines Were Drawn: Remembering Court-Ordered Integration at a Mississippi High School.* Jackson: University Press of Mississippi, 2016.

Hudson, Winson, and Constance Curry. *Mississippi Harmony: Memoirs of a Freedom Fighter.* New York: Palgrave-Macmillan, 2002.

Steele, Alysia Burton. *Delta Jewels: In Search of my Grandmother's Wisdom.* New York: Center Street, 2015.

Sturkey, William, and Jon N. Hale, eds. *To Write in The Light of Freedom: The Newspapers of the 1964 Mississippi Freedom Schools.* Jackson: University Press of Mississippi, 2015.

Tucker, William. *Freedom Summer, A Play about Mississippi in the Summer of 1964.* Tarentum, PA: Word Association Publishers, 2014.

Wilkerson, Isabel. *The Warmth of Other Suns: The Epic Story of America's Great Migration.* New York: Random House, 2010.

# Index

# About the Editors

### Roy DeBerry

Courtesy of Roy DeBerry

A native of Holly Springs, Mississippi, Roy grew up with ten siblings and attended a "Rosenwald" school. He is the executive director and one of the founders of the Hill Country Project. He was active in the civil rights movement in the 1960s, first as a Freedom School student (whose teacher was Hill Country cofounder Aviva Futorian) and then as a general organizer. Roy earned his bachelor's degree in sociology at Brandeis University in 1970. Before continuing education at Brandeis, Roy spent a year studying at the University of Ife, Ile Ife, Nigeria. Back at Brandeis in 1972, he earned a master's degree and later a doctorate in political science in 1978. He has also pursued additional studies at Jackson State University, Duke University, Carnegie-Mellon University, the University of Michigan, and Harvard. He also taught at Rust College, was academic dean at Mississippi Industrial College, both in Holly Springs and Jackson State. Roy is certified to teach at the high school level, and has extensive administrative management experience. Roy believes firmly in education and strongly in a collaboration among education, human service, faith-based organizations, and the business community. He also works to expand parent, community, alumni, and business support for higher education. Active in many community, civic, and professional organizations, Roy has received numerous awards and has been cited for outstanding achievements and contributions. Roy recently retired as vice president for economic development and local governmental affairs at Jackson State University. During his administrative tenure at Jackson State, he also served as executive vice president and vice president of external relations. He has a wife, Rubye, and one daughter, Aisha Isoke.

## Aviva Futorian

Courtesy of Aviva Futorian

Aviva is presently a lawyer in Chicago working on prison reform issues in Illinois, with a focus on long-term prisoners. She grew up in Chicago and received her BA at Brandeis University. She taught high school in Park Forest, Illinois, for three years before coming to Mississippi as part of Freedom Summer. After working as a freedom schoolteacher in the summer of 1964, she became an organizer for the Student Nonviolent Coordinating Committee (SNCC) in Benton County for two years. After leaving Mississippi, she went to law school and received her JD from the University of Chicago, worked as a legislative assistant for Congresswoman Elizabeth Holtzman, became director of the Women's Law Project of the Chicago legal services program, and represented death-sentenced defendants in Illinois in their final appeals. She first met Hill Country Project executive director Roy DeBerry when he was her freedom school student in 1964. They worked together in Benton County in the 1960s, and have both maintained close contact with Benton County residents during the intervening years. Aviva was also among the first organizers to initiate oral history interviews in Benton County in 1995.

## Stephen Klein

Courtesy of Stephen Klein

Stephen worked with the US Agency for International Development from 1963 until he retired in 1990. He began his career working on economic development issues in Africa for fifteen years. He then served as USAID Energy Policy Advisor, and subsequently lived in Morocco for five years where he served as energy policy advisor, assisting Morocco in utilizing its abundant use of solar energy, and improving the efficiency of the country's energy use. Stephen was a member of US delegations for the UN Conference on New and Renewable sources held in Nairobi, Kenya in 1981, and at the UN Conference on Environment and Development (UNCED) held in Rio de Janeiro in 1992. He lives in Washington, DC, where he has been an active participant for many years in community affairs, including mentoring local school children. Stephen attended Cornell University (BA) and the University of Chicago Graduate School of Business (MBA).

### John Lyons

John is an Emmy Award-winning documentary filmmaker and a teaching artist, who has been making films with students in the Chicago area for over nine years. John has worked with young people in the Chicago Public School System, various community arts centers, and Snow City Arts, an arts education organization dedicated to working with hospitalized children. He is a graduate of Columbia College Chicago and currently works at Marwen, a Chicago nonprofit that provides free visual arts education to underserved public school students. His first trip to Mississippi was in the fall of 2003, and he has made over thirty subsequent trips to capture these stories.

Courtesy of John Lyons

Printed in the United States
By Bookmasters